A New Way of Living

By the same author:

POWER FOR THE BODY OF CHRIST

AS AT THE BEGINNING

WALK IN THE SPIRIT

SPIRITUAL WARFARE

NONE CAN GUESS

A New Way of Living

by

MICHAEL HARPER

How the Church of the Redeemer,
Houston, found a new life-style

HODDER AND STOUGHTON
LONDON SYDNEY AUCKLAND TORONTO

Copyright © 1973 by Michael Harper. First printed 1973. This edition 1974. ISBN 0 340 19147 3. All rights reserved. No part of this publication may be reproduced or transmitted in any form or by any means, electronic or mechanical, including photocopy, recording, or any information storage and retrieval system, without permission in writing from the publisher. This book is sold subject to the condition that it shall not, by way of trade or otherwise, be lent, re-sold, hired out or otherwise circulated without the publisher's prior consent in any form of binding or cover other than that in which this is published and without a similar condition including this condition being imposed on the subsequent purchaser. Printed in Great Britain for Hodder and Stoughton Limited, St. Paul's House, Warwick Lane, EC4P 4AH by Richard Clay (The Chaucer Press), Ltd, Bungay, Suffolk.

Contents

To the sons of God
who are the community of the
Church of the Redeemer,
Houston

Foreword

THIS IS AN important book—a book which should be read by many. But it is also a very challenging book. Therefore I do not advise anybody to read it who desires to remain in cosy isolation. The central figure of the book is the Holy Spirit and its purpose is to call the Church to a new understanding of the need for true community—a community in which we are prepared to share our talents, our possessions, and our home.

My reason for writing this foreword is that I have had personal experience of the community described in these pages. Eighteen months ago Graham Pulkingham lectured to the clergy and lay people of my Diocese. When the lectures had been given, he came to tell me he believed that the Holy Spirit was calling him to come to Britain and to work in my Diocese. Today a group of twenty-five people are at work on a housing estate in the City of Coventry. They seem to express more clearly than any group I know, the desires and hopes of a large meeting of lay people who met together recently for a whole day. During their conference they shared the conviction that the world would sit up and take notice of the Church when they saw Christians living out and demonstrating a style of Christian living which was both sacrificial and different in this increasingly affluent society of our day. These lay people wanted to see three things. First, they wanted Christians to hold more lightly to material possessions. Secondly, they wanted Christians to express gaiety; and, thirdly, they wanted Christians to experience a greater togetherness.

I believe that the Pulkingham community are expressing precisely these three things. They are gloriously gay; they are together, living under one roof, sharing all things in common, and, thirdly, they are sitting very lightly to the material things of this world.

From my personal experience of these people, I can commend this book wholeheartedly. I believe that it has an important message, not only to church people in this country, but to the nation as a whole.

APRIL 1973

CUTHBERT COVENTRY

Author's Preface

ALTHOUGH NOT THE easiest of books to write, it has certainly
been the most enjoyable. The book is about the men and
women who make up the fellowship of the Church of the
Redeemer, an Episcopal Church in Houston, Texas, who
have pioneered *a new way of living*.

I want to record my indebtedness to the many friends one
has met in the church itself. Although perhaps invidious to
mention particular people, I should like to thank Graham
Pulkingham, the Rector, for his careful reading of the manuscript and the hours he gave my wife and me when we visited
the church in the winter of 1972. Also the McNeils who
shared their home with us, and kept the freezer well stocked
with ice cream. We are grateful to Mary McCracken who gave
us the keys of her new car so that we might be more mobile
when we were there. We remember Ginger, who developed
and printed my films for me.

I should also like to record my deep gratitude to the Word
of God Community in Ann Arbor, Michigan, a kind of sister
community, who gave me hospitality on the same visit, and for

permission to quote extensively from the *New Covenant*, the monthly magazine of the Catholic charismatic renewal.

I am indebted to Betty Jane Pulkingham for helping to write the last chapter.

Nearer home, I should like to thank my friend and colleague Tom Smail for reading the manuscript, making helpful and encouraging comments and not sparing me when he disagreed. Also Sylvia Lawton, my secretary, who has completed the typing work in record time and efficiency. Jeanne, my wife, is really co-author, for the book has been our companion constantly through 1972, and she has kept me at it with her usual blend of faith and encouragement.

And finally, I should like to record my thankfulness to the publishers—Hodder & Stoughton. I am particularly grateful to Edward England, their religious editor, who has done so much for religious publishing in Britain.

One ought really to thank the readers, but maybe this would be more appropriate at the end rather than the beginning of the book (if you ever get there!). But thank you all the same, particularly for the letters I get from time to time. Now let's get down to business. No-one ever reads prefaces anyway.

MICHAEL HARPER   NEW YEAR'S DAY, 1973

I

Sing me no song

Words, words, words—
I'm sick of words.
Sing me no song
Read me no rhyme
Don't waste my time
Show me.
                    My Fair Lady

ON CHRISTMAS EVE 1972 an old lady of sixty-eight was found
dead in her home in Liverpool. She had choked to death
eating a piece of cardboard. But her death had actually taken
place three months earlier. Other people were living in the
same building. Her family lived close by, and she was well
known to the welfare, housing and pension authorities. Her
neighbours were described as "well-meaning, reasonable
people". She had four sisters all living in Liverpool, apart
from her own two daughters and their families. But for three
months this old lady "disappeared" like a bleep from a radar
screen. She was less fortunate than Eliza Doolittle in the
musical *My Fair Lady*; she had no one to sing her a song,
read her a rhyme or waste her time.

There are many like this old woman. Although their lives
may not end as tragically as hers did, yet they are quite as
lonely. Thousands in our rootless society are unnoticed and
unwanted. We have seen the slow and apparently relentless
corrosion of community life. The move from the fields and
villages to the cities and factories dealt a mortal blow at our

society, from which it has never recovered. Now amongst the affluent and the dispossessed alike there have been further tragic alienations, and most serious of all, the growing breakdown of family life itself. This old woman had a family. But for three months they might as well not have existed.

Eliza Doolittle, the heroine in *My Fair Lady*, was disenchanted with her lessons. She was sick of words. It all seemed a waste of time. She wanted a demonstration. She expresses poignantly the words the world might well address to the Church. "We are sick of sermons, books, discussions, theologies, Bible lectures. We are not interested in hymns, anthems and choruses. Don't spout poetry at us. *Show us*. Give us a demonstration. We want to see action. Words are not enough. Your words make us sick. And we won't listen to you any more."

The Church may be shocked by such outspokenness. God isn't. He has always known that words are not enough. Words have to be "made flesh". So the One who was transcendent and out of reach became touchable. The One who was invisible and inaudible, was seen and heard. "The Word was made flesh and dwelt among us." Christianity is to be for ever a "flesh and blood" manifestation of God to man. Have we not spiritualised most of it away?

The world awaits a fresh manifestation of Christ within His Body, the Church. It is tired of the platitudes and false promises of politicians, the rash dictums of revolutionaries, and the airy-fairy doctrines of theologians. "Show us," the world yells at the Church. "Let us see you do it. Then we'll listen to your words." The world is justified in demanding a demonstration before it will buy what is offered for sale.

This book does not set forth new ideas. It is about an Episcopal church in Houston, Texas, that discovered a new way of living, not a new way of thinking about life. It is about people in "flesh and blood" encounters with each other. It is not a pious book. In many ways it is more controversial than anything one has written about the Holy Spirit and His gifts. The radical nature of this church's approach to life hits

hard at several sacred cows. When a friend read the draft copy
he commented, "If people swallow this, they haven't understood it."

In many ways this is a success story. But whereas in the
United States success is usually a synonym for virtue, in
Britain it is virtuous to fail. Anyone who dares to succeed is
either deluded or an impostor. But success at the Church of
the Redeemer, Houston, should be seen in the context of the
suffering and sacrifice which has gone with it.

The whole concept of community is to many Christians an
ideal well out of reach of all but a few exceptional people.
To others it is a rather dubious concept reserved for religious
cranks and mystics. What the Church of the Redeemer has
been able to demonstrate is that it is well within the range
of most people. They have done for Christian community
what the "do-it-yourself" ideology has done for amateur
house decorators, put it within everyone's reach.

But we must not press the analogy any further. While most
people can wield a paint-brush or hang paper without too
much danger to others, most of us are unsuited to community
living. A radical change in attitude and outlook is necessary
before it will ever work. And if it is attempted without an
understanding of the dangers involved, it can cause hurt and
harm to many. To attempt community is a serious matter.

But having said that, it is equally serious to avoid it because it is difficult. No harm is done if the blinkers are off
and we are prepared to suffer and face the consequences.

The world is waiting. New songs and sermons won't do.
How about a demonstration?

2

Hidden treasure

THERE WERE PATCHES of snow on the ground, but the winter sun was low and warm in our faces as Norman and I drove across the flat Texan plain to Waco. It was February 1966. Cold foggy England had been left behind a few weeks earlier, but it was nippy the day we drove from Dallas. It was not my first visit to the United States. My wife and I had been there the year before. It had been a speaking tour, mostly attending breakfasts, luncheons and dinners, and doing what Americans love to do, mixing religion with hamburgers, sweet rolls and cups of coffee. It had been hot stuff—gatherings of enthusiastic Pentecostal Christians from all kinds of churches, expecting miracles to fall from heaven as plentifully and colourfully as confetti at a church wedding. But we hardly saw inside a church building, and we left the United States asking ourselves the question, "Has the Holy Spirit been excommunicated or something?" The return visit was intended to provide something of an answer, and a book was to be written about this charismatic movement *inside* the churches, if indeed it was there at all.

But the book never got written, and Houston was to blame. The ironic thing was that Houston had not even been on the original schedule. The visit was entirely an afterthought, the result of a bewildering series of "coincidences". In 1965 I had met a Canadian in London who was then living in Texas, and he invited me to visit him when I was next in the States. I did manage to squeeze in a long weekend with him between visits to Los Angeles and Tulsa, Oklahoma, where I was due to speak at the new university founded by Oral Roberts. I was glad for this short gap in an otherwise busy schedule. But even then there were no plans to visit Houston, instead we were heading that afternoon for Waco.

The weather changed the next day. They say in Texas, "If you don't like the weather, wait five minutes—it will change." A warm front moved in bringing heavy and continuous rain, melting the snow and ice. We had a long drive ahead of us across the State of Texas to its neighbour Louisiana. What with the raucous rear engine of the VW and the sound of driving rain, it was a noisy and damp journey. We spent the night at Shreveport. One pined a bit for the Californian sun, and wondered what was in store.

It was then that things began to happen—inexplicably—tantalisingly so. The whole careful plans of the journey went to pieces. "My plans have changed again," I wrote to my wife. It was the first of several alterations in direction. We were supposed to stay longer in Shreveport, but instead on Monday morning headed south for Houston. My friend had called long distance the Rector of a large episcopal church in the city, and had unexpectedly found a night spot for me. The weather changed as unpredictably as our plans. As we headed for Houston the sun came out and the blue sky was covered with powder puff clouds. The church we were going to was called St. John the Divine. My wife and I had met Tom and Doris Sumners, the Rector and his wife, when they were in England the previous year. Tom was well known in the diocese. He had come to the church as Rector in 1940 when it was only a nice thought. Now it had grown under

Tom's wise leadership and become one of the largest Episcopal churches in the United States. Tom had done a good job. He has the added distinction of vanquishing Billy Graham on the golf course!

The plan was to have one night at the Sumners before flying on to Tulsa. We drove to the fashionable suburbs of River Oaks, where Tom's church was situated. But another change in direction was in store. At the house there was a message to call the Oral Roberts University as soon as I arrived. I was soon talking to Tommy Tyson, a Methodist minister, who was then chaplain at the University.

"I'm sorry about this, Michael," Tommy said, "but Oral Roberts has other plans for Tuesday, so we can't have you to speak as arranged."

I wrote that night to Jeanne, my wife, "This seems strange to me, but no doubt the Lord is in it, so I'll now fly to Chicago on Tuesday."

Something strange was going on. I have since learned that when human plans get tangled with God's purposes, all kinds of warning lights flash, and the whole rhythm and stability of life is disturbed. This was what was happening, and it was disconcerting at the time. I called my friend in Chicago on Monday night, only to hear that he had been whisked away suddenly to the East coast, and so could not put me up a day earlier. Next I discovered that all the flights to Chicago were fully booked, so I was well and truly stranded in Houston. My luck seemed to be out, and I must have displayed some of my impatience to my host.

"Never mind," Tom said, "I've got tickets for the Texan rodeo at the Astrodome tonight—why don't you come with us?"

Even bucking bronchos seemed preferable to twiddling one's thumbs. I said I'd discuss it with my friend in case he had other plans.

I dialled my friend's number, and found he was in. We discussed the plans together. I found it difficult to believe that all these changes, cancellations and travelling frustrations were part of God's plan for me to watch a rodeo show.

There was a pause in the conversation, and I knew my friend was weighing alternatives at the other end of the line.

"There is another church here," he said in a rather matter of fact way, "you might be interested, I think." In a city the size of Houston, one really didn't need this kind of information.

"Let me run you over there in the morning—and you can see what you think of it. I think the Rector will be in. It's charismatic, you know," he added, as if I hadn't already guessed it.

So Tuesday morning I was climbing into the VW and we were heading cross town to the mangy suburb of Eastwood. River Oaks stands for the new American prosperity—the rich, white haven for the lucky few. Eastwood represents that side of American life which most people try to forget. But there I stumbled on hidden treasure. And the death knell of my book sounded loud and clear. I wrote home to Jeanne, "The last day has been fascinating. The way the Lord has led has been fantastic. Someone must have been praying back home! God clearly wanted me to stay in Houston for a purpose—I have since discovered a *vital* one."

I had never heard of either the church or its Rector. No-one then seemed to have heard of it either, apart from my friend, of course. We chatted in the car as we drove along the sun drenched freeway.

"It's called the Church of the Redeemer," he informed me, "and its Rector is Graham Pulkingham."

The Eastwood district of Houston is a fairly typical inner-city mix-up. Some years ago it was one of the better places to live in, and only a few miles from down-town Houston. Light industry and residences have grown up cheek by jowl. Railroad tracks criss-cross here and there, and the sound of sirens from the marshalling yards fills the air night and day. Dominating the area is the tall superstructure of the Maxwell House coffee factory, eternally hissing and emitting the pungent odours that make this brand famous throughout the world.

But Houston has sprawled out far beyond Eastwood, and the well-to-do have gone out with the tide, leaving the usual flotsam of humanity on the foreshore, the ever present wreckage of modern society. The whole district has obviously seen better days.

And there, right in the middle, is the Church of the Redeemer, like a great ship stranded high on the shore, the owners of whom are faced with the decision whether to break her up, or try to get her moved down to the sea again.

Graham had just had a shower when he greeted me, with the minimum of fuss and formalities. I was face to face with a quiet man, with a slightly frightening aura about him. He didn't say very much, but seemed to look very intently when he spoke to you, without being rude. One found oneself being rather more careful than usual what one said.

"He was very diffident, and was obviously screening me, asking leading questions and being non-committal himself," was how I described this interview in a letter to Jeanne. I sat opposite him, unashamedly taking notes as we talked, jotting down the things he said which appealed to me. We were interrupted by a down-and-out with a stereotype story.

"Jesus doesn't want you to buy a drink," said Graham, looking the man right in the face. "Besides you'd better go and fetch your friend."

I knew that Graham had not left the room at all during this brief conversation, so he could not have known that there was a confederate lurking in the background. The man looked a little stunned, and I noticed that "I-perceive-that-you-are-a-prophet" expression on his face.

The incident passed, and we talked on. Graham told me his story. He related how he had come to the church in the first place. He had to learn many bitter lessons about failure. Then came his baptism in the Spirit. He returned to the hopeless situation and began to see miracles taking place before his very eyes.

Graham switched from subject to subject. He painted the demoralising picture of the area where they were living. I remember him telling me about the new youthful fad of glue-sniffing, then growing in popularity. My pen raced across the paper, catching some of the more important and thought provoking statements, such as—

"We were typical Anglicans—hearty, cold and proud."

"America has become very religious—but it's soulish religion, not spiritual."

"So much evangelism is like a bodyless arm; there is a reaching out, but no body to sustain the new life."

"The subtle deception of the carnal Christian Church is more dangerous than communism."

We shared views about the charismatic revival. Graham was typically phlegmatic—

"I've had to deal with too many casualties."

"There are too many with a Pentecostal experience, but with whole blocks of their lives untouched by God."

"The prayer meeting can become just like another country club activity—a glossolalia club."

I wrote to Jeanne, "I think we were beginning to click."

"Why don't you come on over and speak at the church meeting tonight," Graham said just before we left. The Texan rodeo didn't stand a chance.

We met in a rather dingy basement of the church house. I don't remember very much about it, apart from the fact that it was quite well attended. We had supper beforehand with the inner core of the church fellowship. A man called Jeff cooked the meal for us. He had just been drawn into the church after being bailed out of prison through the influence of one of the church members. From prison he had been taken into one of the household communities, which were just being started at that time. Jeff was just finding his feet, and when we came back six years later we discovered that he had blossomed into being one of the leaders of the church. All I remember then was that he knew how to cook.

I do remember that when I came to speak there was a warm response from those who were listening. Jeff himself told me six years later that my words had been a confirmation to them at the time that what they were doing was on the right lines. I gathered that they had taken me as being some kind of a prophet, speaking to their situation without knowing beforehand exactly what it was.

"Graham's face was a picture," Jeff told me, "he looked kinda relieved," as if it had been an endorsement from God that they were going in the right direction.

At that time I was having to learn that charismatic meetings in the United States do not know when to terminate. This one was no exception, for when half the gathering drifted off home, the rest packed into a tiny prayer chapel in the basement of the church, and we were there until well after midnight. It was these few hours which finally convinced me that I had stumbled on a very unusual kind of church. I felt I had something really good to write about.

The meeting in that small chapel that night impressed itself indelibly on my memory. It was hauntingly memorable. The people there obviously knew each other extremely well. There was no sense of rush about what was happening. One felt that two contradictory things were happening, at first sight it was as if they had worked it all out carefully before they had started, and yet at the same moment, it was as if everything they said and did was new and fresh to them. There was an economy about it all. No time was being wasted. Some were prayed for as needs were expressed. Each person came forward and knelt at the altar rail. A tiny knot of people grouped themselves around the person. Hands were laid on them. Clear and appropriate words were spoken—the person nodding their head in approval. God was there. A gentle peace pervaded the chapel. No-one was in a hurry. There was no heavy hand of leadership, yet Graham was very obviously the leader. It was so clear that an unseen power was guiding the whole business.

"The Lord has given me a scripture," a woman told us, her tone of voice expressing partly excitement, partly mystery. "The words are very strange," she said.

"Never mind." said Graham, "let's hear them."

"They're from Leviticus," she said—"thou shalt not uncover thy sister's nakedness."

There was a pause, no-one knowing quite what to say. The strangeness of the words stunned everyone into silence.

"I reckon God is saying something here about our church," said Graham slowly. "God is saying that we are not to seek for or allow any publicity for the moment. This is a work of God which should not be uncovered."

My heart gave a bit of a lurch. I could see a good story slipping from my grasp.

"We have a reporter here," went on Graham. "These words refer to you, Michael," he said, turning and smiling at me.

So the book was never written. The wisdom of that decision to hide this young work from the prying eyes of the rest of the Church has been confirmed again and again. A leak at that stage would have been disastrous. But the story can now be told without embarrassing anyone. The fact, however, that the work was able to go on without the glare of publicity was an important factor in its successful development.

Just before I left Houston Graham said to me, "We have no story yet, we are only beginning."

From 1966 until September 1969 Graham stayed put in Houston, barely moving out of the city limits.

"The one thing wrong with this place," he had remarked to me in 1966, "it's so time consuming." But from the fall of 1969 he has been more often away from the church than there. By then the foundations had been well and truly laid. A test of any live church is how long it will survive without its leader. The Church of the Redeemer has more than survived, it has actually thrived while Graham has been away.

Next morning I left for Chicago. Tom and Doris drove me to the airport. I had difficulty changing my ticket, and the minutes ticked away. I would not have minded that much if I had missed the plane. I nearly did anyway. I was the last passenger to embark, and the engines were started as I sprinted up the gangway. Graham also came out to the airport to see me off. I sensed he wanted me back in Houston, as he slipped me a bundle of dollar bills, the offering they had taken for me.

"Just enough for your ticket back from Chicago," he said, grinning at me. On the flight to Chicago I wrote to Jeanne, "I'm wondering if the Lord does want me back there. We are both praying about this—and He will lead."

He did—but six years were to pass before I went back. On this occasion my wife Jeanne accompanied me. Graham had come to Britain in 1971 at our invitation. He was perfectly happy this time that something should be written up about the Church of the Redeemer, and was himself at the time writing *Gathered for Power*—his first book.[1]

The plane we caught at Kennedy airport was the milk plane, as it is sometimes called. It stopped several times on its way to Houston. When we left Nashville, Tennessee, our last stopping place, every seat was taken on the flight. Chatting to the man sitting next to us we discovered that the annual homemakers convention was meeting in the massive Astrodome that week, hence the large number of prosperous looking businessmen on this particular flight. We were going on a very different kind of homemakers excursion.

It was the end of January 1972, almost exactly six years after the last visit. Although the foundations had been laid, there was not much of a visible structure back in 1966. But now there was very much more to see, and the cat was out of the bag all right.

At the end of 1969 *Time* magazine did its traditional crystal-ball gazing into the future, looking hard at the America of the '70s. In the religious section they selected three viable models for the coming decade, and one of them was the coffee house ministry of the Church of the Redeemer.

Next year Madeline Karr-Amgott was commissioned by the Columbia Broadcasting Service (CBS) to do a TV religious special on "the Jesus people", which was then catching the headlines in the United States. They contacted Graham Pulkingham, and asked if they could come down and do some filming as a part of this special programme. But when they eventually arrived in Houston they were so impressed with what they saw of the church that they decided to devote the whole film to it, and they called it *Following the Spirit*. The film was eventually shown on Whitsunday 1971, and seen throughout the United States on the CBS network.

The producer, Ted Holmes, described the church enthusiastically as "the most exciting and vital example of the new religious way to be found in the country today. These people, receiving together, working together, have dedicated themselves to the ministries of the church. It is not a commune—a commune implies dropping out. The fellowship members have not turned their backs on society. On the contrary they are trying to make changes in society at large and particularly in the Houston area, by setting an example for others to follow."

They were fortunate in having one of the best camera crews in the United States when the film was actually made. Camera crews work in teams, and union regulations are such that if one member is missing, the whole team breaks up. On the day the CBS producers arrived in Houston the local crew had to disband, as one member dropped out because of bereavement in the family. An urgent call was put through to Hollywood for a replacement, and it so happened there was one crew free at that time. It also "happened" to be one of the best in the United States, used to filming some of the top TV programmes like the Frank Sinatra show. They were flown specially from Hollywood and the film that resulted is a tribute to their technical skill.

"We hardly had time to clean our teeth before they arrived," cracked Graham when he told me that they had only been given twelve hours notice. So one sees on the film the real thing—unvarnished and unrehearsed.

From the early 1970s the accolades have come thick and fast. *American Church News* called the church "a vital parish such as is seldom found in the Anglican Communion. They value 'speaking in tongues' as an important witness of the Spirit's work, but they do not exalt this gift out of proportion to the rest of the Gospel. On the contrary the parish is more Eucharist-centred than many Anglican churches and their dedication to social action is phenomenal."

Father Jim Scheyer, a Roman Catholic priest from Virginia, Minnesota, wrote after his first visit to the church,

"The Church of the Redeemer has had a most profound influence on my way of thinking as a Christian, as a Catholic and as a Catholic priest. How do I describe the Redeemer experience? For me it is an experiencing of 'the body of Christ' ... A believing Christian finds the experience of Jesus Christ very real and tangible when observing and participating in the love that the members of a parish family like the Redeemer church have for one another."

When Dr. George Macleod, founder of the Iona Community, visited the church in 1972, he wrote about it, "A living fellowship of faith every bit as Pentecostal as Pentecost itself ... Here indeed is witness to 'all things in common' to an extent that probably exceeds the achievement of the early Pentecostal Church."

Each year *Guideposts* magazine presents a "Church Award". It is one of America's leading religious magazines. It was founded by Norman Vincent Peale, and its editors include Leonard LeSourd, husband of Catherine Marshall, and John Sherrill, author of several religious best-sellers. The Award for 1972 went to the Church of the Redeemer. The citation runs: "The group experience is very likely this church's most significant achievement, among a host of remarkable achievements. They hold firmly to the idea of a strong parish church ... the Christian life is meant to be a corporate experience ... by their example, the members of the congregation of the Church of the Redeemer are strengthening the concept of church, the concept of a body of believers. Their strong, innovative, practical, faithful example gives hope and help to churches everywhere."

Church Awards or TV Religious Specials are not necessarily signs of the Kingdom of God. But in eight years an

Episcopal church has defied all the normal facts of ecclesiastical life. Existing in a changing inner city area—it has not, like most other churches, moved out to the prosperous suburbs. Nor has it become the beneficiary of funds from outside bodies determined to do "a good thing" in a socially unacceptable district. Nor has it experienced a kind of "artificial insemination". Most churches cop out when faced with this situation. In the United States this means closing the church down. In Britain, the parish system of the Anglican Church does not allow such drastic treatment. Yet the inner-city areas of our cities are weakly supported and inadequately staffed. But the traffic flow at the Church of the Redeemer changed direction, and Christians *moved from the suburbs into the inner city*, a reversal of the normal trend.

In eight years the church has undergone an astonishing metamorphosis. When Graham Pulkingham went there in 1963 there was a staff of three—the Rector and two sextons, whose ministry consisted of working 24 hour shifts to protect the church property from vandalism. Apart from church services, very little went on in the life of the church, and its ministry to the neighbourhood was almost non-existent. It was an island in a sea of human need. In 1963 the church had about 900 people on its books, two-thirds of whom were confirmed communicants, but the majority of these people were inactive, so far as the vital life of the church was concerned, since they lived for the most part in the distant suburbs—the white havens of respectability.

By 1971 the church was so changed as to bear little resemblance to what it had been before. The church roll in 1971 reached 1400, *1300 of whom* were active church members. Only about half of these are confirmed members of the Episcopal Church, which suggests an interesting grassroots ecumenism. But most significant of all, for in the changing patterns of modern living there are probably other examples of dynamic church growth in the Western world, the figures show a complete reversal of the common pattern of inner-city abandonment. Over 150 families have moved into Houston's East End to live close to the church, and thus share more fully the corporate life of Christian fellowship and also minister freely where Christ is not known and where His love and grace is most needed. The financial situation has also changed radically in eight years. In 1963 income was less than $40,000, and the church was heading for bankruptcy and an early closure. By 1971 income had risen to $220,000, and since 1967 there have been no pledge cards or canvasses of membership to raise funds.

At the same time the staff of the church has grown to four ordained men and thirty full-time lay persons. Average weekly attendance at services in the church is around 2200. How all this has come about is quite a story.

3

A people prepared

And he will turn many of the sons of Israel to the Lord their God, and he will go before him in the spirit and power of Elijah, to turn the hearts of the fathers to the children, and the disobedient to the wisdom of the just, to make ready for the Lord a people prepared.

Luke 1: 16-17

GRACE WASN'T SURE whether her prayer had been answered or not. She had been a member of the Church of the Redeemer for several years, when something happened to change her way of life. She was baptised in the Spirit. This experience, for many years the virtual monopoly of the Pentecostals, began to come to Episcopalians and members of other Churches during the 1950s and 1960s. For the most part the experiences were confined to a few in each church, and Grace found herself isolated and misunderstood in the Church of the Redeemer. Some of her friends counselled her to quit the church and join a more sympathetic group, but Grace had learned to listen to the Holy Spirit rather than people, and the word she had was "stay and pray".

But she wasn't too sure whether Graham Pulkingham, the new Rector of the church, was the answer to her prayers or not. People who knew him in those days described him as "a cold intellectual". He had been born in Alliance, Ohio, the second child of Canadians from Hamilton, Ontario. He was brought up a Roman Catholic, baptised and confirmed in that Church, and remained a member until he was twenty-five, when he joined the Episcopal Church. He was married to Betty Jane, the daughter of a superior court judge, Leo Carr of Burlington, North Carolina.

He received varied training before his ordination in 1957. He has a BA degree from the University of Western Ontario. Then for three years studied music under Dr. Roy Harris. Then he had two years in seminary followed by three years in the United States Navy. He completed his seminary training with a BD degree. After ordination he served in two parishes and then became Chaplain at the University of Texas Medical School in Galveston. From 1960 to 1963 he served under Charles Sumners, whose twin brother Tom was the Rector of St. John the Divine, the first church I visited in Houston in 1966. While Chaplain at medical school he served in an experimental health team, which was set up through a grant received from the American National Mental Health Society. The team studied "multiple impact therapy" which is mainly concerned with the rehabilitation of troubled adolescents, and the background of the problems of community sicknesses.

The most vocal of the senior members of the Church of the Redeemer knew which way the church was going. By all accounts it was doomed to early extinction. A new and younger Rector would make little difference. The only hope, so they believed, was to make the church a centre for Anglo-Catholic worship. By providing certain frills dear to the hearts of some Episcopalians, it might act as a bait to make it worth their while travelling so far to attend. The Episcopal Cathedral in down-town Houston was not satisfying that need, so the Church of the Redeemer could be made a mecca for pure Anglo-Catholicism in the diocese.

But Graham Pulkingham had other ideas. To him the church should serve the neighbourhood, not be a kind of mass-station for aesthetically deprived Anglo-Catholics. From the start there was a sharp clash between the Rector and his vestrymen. The last straw for some came when the Rector went away on holiday and arranged for a black priest to take the services. The church began to lurch ominously towards its predicted end.

Graham's policy was bold and adventurous. Instead of protecting the property from the neighbours, he threw down the gauntlet, and saw to his increasing horror the property being systematically torn to pieces. Windows were broken and to this day one can see the pock-marked ceilings through which undisciplined youths poked their billiard cues. With total disaster staring him in the face, Graham reluctantly and sadly closed the door on the neighbours, and the church, without the support of its former members and totally failing to reach its neighbours, moved to the very brink of the grave.

It was then that the now desperate Rector, broken and tearful, heard about that classic religious paperback, *Cross and the Switchblade*, which tells the story of a young Pentecostal pastor who was faced with a similar situation, in even tougher circumstances. David Wilkerson found a way through the hard asphalt jungle of Brooklyn, New York. Although Graham never read the book, it introduced him to the work which David had developed, in which many young toughs and derelicts of society found deliverance from vicious crime and drugs through the influence of the Holy Spirit. Graham was the sort of person who would do anything and go anywhere to find a solution to the kind of situation he was then facing. He determined as soon as possible to visit Dave Wilkerson and see for himself.

A visit to his wife's parents in North Carolina soon presented him with the opportunity he was looking for, and he was able to sneak off for a few days and drive North to New York City. Graham's first attempt to see Dave Wilkerson ended in failure. He was not used to being kept waiting, and petulantly stamped out of the offices of Teen Challenge. But his need was greater than his pride, so swallowing that, he went and tried again.

Dave Wilkerson's first impressions were not too favourable. "Graham Pulkingham represented to me all that turned me off, in a minister," he said later. But he was prepared to put this man to the test. That night he took him out on the streets to some of the worst parts of Brooklyn. And he saw Graham weep. It was all Graham could do, as he saw horrors which made Houston seem like a Victorian tea party in comparison.

So Wilkerson laid hands on this man, and prayed for him, and Graham received the power of the Spirit. Nothing happened at the time; there were no tongues of fire, nor did he at the time speak in tongues. But when he returned to Houston the difference was immediate and dramatic.

"Next Sunday's services will be as usual..." are words many congregations hear, and services live up to it. But although the services had their usual liturgical pattern, unusual things immediately began to happen in them. A woman came hobbling up to the altar rail on her crutches; Graham had seen people do this before. But this time he stretched out his hand and touched her in the name of Christ. She promptly turned round and walked back to her place leaving her crutches behind. Graham found that the Bible, very little of which he had studied before, became a new book which he read avidly every day. Soon after he came back he found a steady trickle of people coming to him for counsel and help. He found the Holy Spirit was now giving him an authority and new ability to understand and deal with their problems.

Grace knew now that her prayers had been answered. It really had been the Holy Spirit who had told her "stay and pray". Now she knew the reason why.

It is still a comparatively unusual thing for a minister of one of the historic churches to get involved in Pentecostal experiences. But it is no longer a novelty. The Church of the Redeemer could have gone the way of other churches in the charismatic movement. A revived minister gets a group of enthusiasts around him, Pentecostal meetings are held, attended by people from many churches. They become a kind of spiritual "waifs and strays" society, a club for Christian orphans. Good though many of the individual testimonies have been to pentecostal power and blessing, the corporate expressions of these have been on the whole disappointing.

But the Church of the Redeemer chose another way. Neither the Rector nor its congregation became closely associated with the nationwide charismatic movement. They all got their heads down to work out in the nitty-gritty world of today what it really means to be the Body of Christ. They were happy enough to be unknown and at times misunderstood—to be hidden, while God unravelled the mysteries of the Kingdom to them. There is a good French proverb—"recuiller pour sauter mieux"; it is derived from the horseman, who pulls his steed back in order that it may then jump the obstacle more cleanly. In other words he doesn't rush the fences. That is how this church began to tick.

When I visited the church in 1966 they had been spending eighteen months laying deep foundations. Without these strong and sure foundations it would never have developed as strongly as it later did.

The composition of any church is *people*, for the church is people. The church is not a place to worship in, nor an institution or organisation which tells other people what to do, nor a system of thought or a code of morals, it is a body of people whose head is Christ and who function in obedience to Him and in co-operation with each other.

This church came alive and began to develop powerful and varied ministries, all within the frame-work of the Episcopal Church and with the Bishop's full knowledge and approval, when the Rector discovered the source of spiritual power, *and how to share it in fellowship with others*. Unfortunately some who discover the power never seem to learn how to share it. But this is only one side of it; for however willing the minister may be to share with others, lay people also should be willing and free to share in that ministry. The gap between pulpit and pew is not an easy one to bridge.

In the Church of the Redeemer "sharing the ministry" means much more than it does in the average church today.

It represents a total giving of oneself to others, as well as to God.

Between August and October 1964 the Lord began to gather the people who were to form the nucleus of the fellowship of the church. One of the first whom Graham talked to when he returned to Houston from New York was Dr. Bob Eckert, a medical doctor whom he had known since medical school. Bob at first laughed at Graham's story and gave some clever psychological explanations. But then he took him seriously, and a short time later was baptised in the Spirit himself. At the time he was a partner of a successful firm of doctors in a suburb of Galveston, a sea port on the gulf of Mexico, about thirty-five miles from Houston. The Eckerts and Pulkinghams began to see more and more of each other.

Another family that linked up at this time was Jerry and Esther Barker and their five children. Jerry and Esther had been converted through the help of E. Stanley Jones in 1954. But in 1963 they went through a time of great difficulty, especially when Esther was hospitalised with a serious mental illness, which threatened to keep her institutionalised for the rest of her life. At this point Jerry came to the end of his resources.

"I'm not going to try to come up with my own answers any longer," he told the Lord, "if you don't speak to my heart and tell me what to do, I'm not going to do anything."

He was walking home from the hospital when he prayed these words; and immediately had a strong sense of the power and presence of God, which enabled him to begin at once to thank God for healing his wife. Later he discovered that he had been baptised in the Spirit, although at the time he had not realised it. Within the next few days he was to experience some of the gifts of the Spirit. Jerry was a successful attorney in his father's well established Galveston practice. Some of his clients were flabbergasted by the revelations he shared with them concerning themselves and their problems. Esther's healing took place about eighteen months later, and in the meantime all their five children were baptised in the Spirit. The Barkers also linked up with the Eckerts.

The fourth family to be drawn in was the Fields. Ladd and June were members of a Methodist Church in Pasadena, Texas. Ladd was working as an engineer with a firm that makes precision instruments for the oil field industry. In September 1963 he had been shaken out of complacency by attending a laymen's retreat in central Texas, when the atmosphere had become like an old-fashioned revival. The Lord met with them both and gave them a longing for deeper fellowship in the Body of Christ. The baptism in the Spirit came later, the fruit of a dream Ladd had. Later they were led to Houston, where they were drawn into the close fellowship of the nucleus of the church. Again it was a dream that was the main source of their guidance. Ladd woke up in the middle of the night and heard the Lord say "Go to the Church of the Redeemer".

The Grimmets were the fifth family. John had worked for the local power company as a foreman electrician for twenty-five years. He had been a member of the Church of the Redeemer for many years, and also on the vestry.

The nucleus was completed by three women, Nancy Carr, Graham Pulkingham's wife's sister, Alice West and Arabella Miner.

All these people, husbands, wives and children, made the Redeemer Church their home, except for Ladd Fields, who remained in his Methodist Church until Palm Sunday 1965. From October 1964 they began to meet regularly every Tuesday night.

There was something mysterious about why these particular people were drawn together, but there was nothing strange about what went on when they found themselves becoming an integrated body of people. Right from the start the story of the church is basically about *groups* rather than individuals.

There is no hero, no superstar. They were all in it together.

Each family moved into Houston only when they had heard God speak. They were all hard-working members of society, mostly working eighteen hours a day. They were not opting out of society in search of some esoteric experience. There was from the start a total giving to each other, and there were no differences in status. Graham, the Rector, and his wife Betty, were as much involved in this self-giving as the others. And there was no distinction made between male and female. The women were as much accepted as part of this team ministry as the men.

"The Lord put within our hearts an urgency to be together," is how Jerry Barker has described it. The Lord began to spoil them, "Practically anything we would pray for was answered almost instantly. All kinds of wild things would happen in our lives."

They began to share in every way possible. Jerry describes how they would dive to each others' homes, "When we got there, we'd pull out our Bibles and sit around the kitchen table or something like that and just start sharing what the Lord had been showing us and what had been happening in our personal lives. We'd just be awed at His majesty and grace, and we couldn't get over what He was doing to us."

During Lent 1965 the group began to study the Acts of the Apostles, and were immediately struck by the account in the second chapter of the way the Spirit-filled Church shared so fully and completely together. The Lord impressed upon them all, that He wanted them to live this life together. It is described in Acts in this way: "They met *constantly* to hear the apostles teach, and to share the common life, to break bread and to pray. A sense of awe was everywhere, and many marvels and signs were brought about through the apostles. All whose faith had drawn them together held everything in common: they would sell their property and possessions and make a general distribution as the need of each required..." (Acts 2: 42-45 NEB)

Easter 1965 was a crucial time for this tiny embryonic community. On Good Friday the Lord told several of the group that they were to begin meeting at 5.30 every week-day morning for prayer, even if they were not yet living together. On Easter Monday the first early morning meeting was held. Their guidance was sealed by a remarkable occurr-ence, for Alice West, who for some reason or other had not been informed of this meeting, had such a strong impression from the Lord that she got up early on Easter Monday and travelled ten miles across town to pray in the chapel, and was surprised to find a meeting, when she arrived at the same time as the others did! This was confirmation enough that they were on the right tracks and becoming the kind of group that could truly function and be led by the Spirit *together*.

On May 1 another big step was taken. The three single women, Nancy Carr, Alice West and Arabella Miner moved into a house near the church. Apart from the Pulkinghams, who of course lived in the Rectory next door to the church property, this was the first of the household communities to be set up by someone in the fellowship. Others were soon to follow. Dr. Eckert and his family moved from Alta Loma on June 1st and ten days later the Barkers from Galveston. In August the Fields and Grimmets moved to within a few blocks of the church.

Both Bob Eckert and Jerry Barker relocated their medical and legal practices in Houston. Their great desire was to be as close together as possible. "Any house we could get that was close was suitable," is how Jerry puts it. They didn't care what it looked like. They all came from big and luxurious homes, but that didn't matter any more. The over-riding concern was to share life together. "It was just like a kid on Christmas Eve, we were expecting anything," is how Jerry has described their experience.

Ladd Fields kept his job, as he could work from his new home near the church; so did John Grimmet, although later he left it to become head maintenance man at the church, in charge of the repair work that was necessary at the time.

For the next three years an interesting pattern developed. The Lord taught them how to relate to one another as *brothers*, before He taught them how to relate as *neighbours*. It sounds simple enough, but it was a profound and far reaching discovery. Only when they had become a closely knit fellowship and had developed an "eye-ball to eye-ball" relationship were they able to function properly as ambassadors for Christ. For three years this church did very little about evangelism. The Lord took care of all that, and sent people to them who were in need, without their having to go out at all. The word got out that the Church of the Redeemer was a place where people could get help, and outsiders found a settled open-ended fellowship of people who had the time and the compassion to help them, rather than a phrenetic bunch of individuals feverishly doing their "witnessing thing".

The news got around that the Church of the Redeemer was not dying after all, and a steady trickle of people came to see the "great thing that had come to pass". They were asked "What are you doing?" Their truthful answer was "nothing". Self-styled prophets criticised them—"You must get out and evangelise," they were told. "You will die if you do not evangelise," they were warned. Fortunately they took no notice, but politely assured these people that God had said something quite different to them. They had three years of intensive fellowship, during which God taught them how to minister to needs such as alcoholism, drug addiction, prostitution, demon possession, sexual perversion, mental and emotional illness by actually sending people with such needs to them. Then they were told to "go". But that was some years later.

When the Barkers moved into the neighbourhood of the church, three troubled men moved in with them. One was a con man, another an epileptic who had immense and potentially dangerous physical strength even when sedated. The other man was a harmless schizophrenic. All of them are now stabilised. One of them is a leader of the church, another helps with the maintenance work and the third has left Houston and is a member of a Christian group in Dallas.

An alcoholic moved in with the three women. Arabella Miner stopped work, and has been full-time in the church ever since. Alice West left work in June of the same year. Arabella and Alice, to begin with, became fully occupied with the rehabilitation programme for those who had been sent to them.

The Barkers' household began to grow. One or two younger men joined them, who had just become committed Christians and been baptised in the Spirit. Within no time at all seven other people were added to the family.

They started at once to live a community life. The men moved upstairs with the Barkers two older boys. The rest of the children and Jerry and Esther lived downstairs. Their meals were eaten together and they shared their lives. "It was a community from the day we moved in," is the way Jerry himself has put it. "This was true of the other houses too. It was just the natural thing to do." People came to them with deep needs, and they knew they couldn't help them unless they were prepared to take them right into their own lives. They used to say to these people, "Come on over and live with us and believe the Lord with us."

The newly formed community found itself at times in desperate situations. For instance one of the mental cases would sometimes get violent. All they did was to cry to the Lord to restrain him. Immediately the man found himself stuck as if by glue to a chair, unable to move. He was literally bound there as if an angel was holding him down, and he hadn't so much as been touched.

These people also began to share their resources, and particularly to help those members of their household who had no money of their own. Whenever there was any material need, it was natural to share it. When someone, for instance, needed furniture, it was shared. If it was a car—then that too was given or shared.

Each of them began to live a life of simplicity. They stopped buying new cars and televisions. Possessions were of value only for their usefulness to the community. They began to turn in their insurance policies. The new community found such a security in its relationship with the Lord and with each other that it no longer seemed important to have security for the future or protection against possible disasters. But they made no rules about it, nor did they regard it as a necessary part of Christian living, it was just something the Lord had told them to do. These people learned to live more economically. T-bone steaks and expensive roasts were "out". Sometimes they had nothing in the house and someone would arrive with a box of groceries from nowhere, or a sack of rice.

The wives and children were very much part of the community life and joined in the ministry of the household. It drew the families together more closely than they had known before. When they had really difficult mentally sick people living with them, it was sometimes necessary for them to arrange twenty-four hour shifts, so that they were never left alone. The older children would volunteer for this, and so learn how to be part of the ministry of the household and how to care for troubled people.

These households became Christian communities open and vulnerable to the frustrated households around them. They became servants of God. Although they were all lay-men, they shared in the total ministry of the church as fully as Graham himself did. They were called to lay everything aside to serve the Lord in whatever way He indicated.

The single people spent their whole day at the church, praying before breakfast, studying in the mornings, eating together and working during the afternoons. This nucleus of dedicated people constantly visited each other's homes. They met every morning at 6.30 for prayer and Communion, and every evening for fellowship at 7.30, sometimes going on into the early hours of the morning. They seldom let each other out of sight, even spending the weekends together.

During the summer of 1966 the girls made curtains for the Barkers' house and cooked the evening meal for all the families. The boys re-roofed the house and painted the outside of it. Meanwhile Jerry Barker was becoming so committed to the work of the church that he became a full-time worker and assistant pastor of the church. He was heavily involved in teaching and counselling. Later he was to go back into legal practice, and set up a free legal aid clinic in the 4th Ward of the city, part of the black ghetto.

All of the five original families gave themselves unqualifiedly to service. "We really had no private life; we didn't want any," was how one of them described it. "We ministered the Lord's life at meal times, we ministered during the evening and sometimes we got up in the middle of the night to minister." Jerry Barker tells how "Some of the best and most dependable ministers I had in my house were my three older children. You could absolutely depend upon them in critical situations. It was tremendous to see this happening in teenagers."

One of the most inhibiting factors in many churches, preventing them from functioning properly, is the position or status of the minister. However open people may be— there is still a crippling self-consciousness amongst the laity in face of the professional, and reluctance to function freely as members of the Body of Christ. Graham Pulkingham was well aware of this. He has a strong personality and it usually takes considerable sang-froid for lay people to minister when he is around. There is at least one easy and simple answer— move away! Throughout this three year period of intensive "fellowshipping" those involved had not even taken vacations, as they did not want to be separated from each other. But during the summer of 1967 the group sensed that God was calling them to a new stage in the life of the church. Graham took a two month vacation, taking his family, Nancy Carr and Arabella Miner, two of the single women, and Bill Farra, who had recently joined the church after the death of his wife very shortly after their marriage. Graham realised that the best way the church could begin to function fully was to withdraw himself, so that the laity could begin to pull their weight. His absence worked wonders.

When they got back they decided that the time had come for the "church family", the inner nucleus that had been drawn so close together, to break up, and for the individual households to become the real centre for ministry to the people the Lord was continuing to send to the church for help.

Gradually new patterns developed. In the summer of 1968 a priest came to the church, Jeff Schiffmayer, and he was later to become the pastor of the church. At the same time Dr. Bob Eckert set up a medical clinic in the black ghetto of Houston. Outreach was beginning to be one of the ministries of the church. 1968 was a year in which the Lord told them many times that he was about to send them out, whereas before He had told them to be together and have all things in common, to share their possessions and their lives, to open their houses and hearts to one another; now He was beginning to say, "Go out and share your life with the world." In the meantime He had been training them in dealing with the troubled people who had been coming to them for help. They were a trained, instructed, united body of people, who knew what it meant in practical and personal terms to lay down their lives for one another.

In the autumn of 1968 the Pulkinghams left the Rectory and moved into a derelict house in the North Main Street, right next to the railroad yards. It was a kind of symbol of the "moving out" of the church in terms of evangelism and social action. The house was in a very dilapidated condition, needing complete remodelling. Much of it had been eaten away by termites. It took nine months to set right, but it was to become the centre for the youth outreach.

In 1969 eleven members of the church travelled to New York to train in street evangelism. Others stayed behind and turned the garage of the North Main house into a coffee house. "The Way In" was the name given to the new youth ministry which opened on July 4, 1969. That September Graham Pulkingham and Bill Farra left for their first "apostolic" journey. It lasted three months. From 1970 onwards

Graham and Bill were away from the church for up to eighty
per cent of the time in a ministry which has taken them
around the world, right across North America, to Britain
in 1971 and 1972; and to New Zealand also. When Graham
returned to Houston in 1971 to write his first book, Bill
travelled to Auckland, New Zealand, where he worked alongside Archdeacon Kenneth Prebble, Vicar of St. Paul's, a
church in which a new and powerful ministry is developing.

The expansion since 1969 has been dramatic. In addition
to the coffee house work and the medical and law clinics
already mentioned, a ranch has been obtained in the heart of
Texas and is used as a rehabilitation centre for addicts. A
shop selling religious books and gifts has been opened in a
prosperous suburb. Literacy work has been started and a
community opened in the hippy district. Another racially
mixed community has started in the worst part of the black
ghetto, and there are over forty other household communities, all catering for the needs of people around them. Prison
visiting is a regular and fruitful part of the work of the
church. The facts speak for themselves.

A revolution has taken place which not only has brought
revival to a church which most people thought was doomed,
but now brings renewal to churches everywhere. All this
has been happening at a time when the Church at large is
having to face a serious crisis. Perhaps this is no coincidence.

4

Is there an answer?

Tell me why?
Is there an answer?
            Hair

THE CHURCH, LIKE the world in which it lives, is facing a crisis of terrifying proportions. The salt is losing its savour, the fires are burning low. Leaving apart for the moment the crisis of faith, the Church is suffering from unprecedented stress, and the signs are ominous in several vital areas. In the first place there is a chronic manpower shortage. Men and women have not been coming forward for full-time ministry in anything like the numbers necessary to maintain the *status quo*, let alone cope with the heavier demands of modern society. Ordination figures for the Church of England are declining. For example, the total ordained in 1971 was less than 400, the lowest figure since 1949. Although amalgamations and various rationalisation schemes have put off the evil day, the hour is fast approaching when there may well be a dangerous and impossible situation, with many churches hopelessly understaffed, and some depleted altogether of clergy. The ordaining of part-time clergy has been one way of dealing with the crisis, but at the moment it seems a case of "too few and too late" to make much difference to the coming crisis.

Trends in other churches are if anything worse. Churches are closing down in many parts of Britain. In the United States the post-war religious boom, which made "religion" one of the largest areas of business expansion, seems to be levelling off, and in the Roman Catholic church there is a serious manpower shortage, with fewer than ever going into the religious orders. Hans Kung writes in his book *Why Priests?*, "The loss rate and, above all, the decline in vocations not only in North and South America but in Europe are clear evidence that the crisis is approaching disaster point."[2]

Linked with the manpower shortage is the comparative failure in lay apostolate. The Church has been saying for many years that the laity should take a full and active part in church affairs. The movement in the Church of England towards synodical government has had this aspect much in mind, in getting the laity more fully involved in the government of the Church. But in practical terms the laity have not fully risen to the occasion, especially in local church situations, and also in the area of ministry to people, which is so important for the future. The role of the laity continues to be largely administrative. Ministers are guilty too of unwillingness to allow laity a full and active part in preaching, teaching, counselling and caring for people's composite needs. The burden for this still rests heavily on ministers, who are also expected to do far too much administrative work.

Allied with manpower problems are financial difficulties. In the United States, for instance, the Episcopal Church has been facing financial crises. In Britain the closure of churches and the running down of the ministry is partly accounted for by the Church's failure to keep pace with galloping inflation. The future looks even more gloomy. Much of the Church's time and effort is spent in fund raising and dealing with the increasingly complex affairs arising from spiralling costs and diminishing returns. The machinery of the Church is largely out-of-date and wasteful in terms of labour and, therefore, costs. Buildings, often only used once a week and uneconomical to keep up, are a constant drain on finances. As the standard of living rises, so the Church is being stretched beyond its financial resources in providing adequate stipends and remuneration for its dwindling corps of workers. The church, like John Brown's body, "lies amouldering in the grave", but unlike Brown, it seems its soul is dying there also. Many people—especially ministers, are becoming disillusioned with the present situation, which seems to be deteriorating annually.

But the Church's ills do not end there. There are also grave problems, to some extent arising from what has already been written, in connection with the deployment of the Church's diminishing labour forces, and to some extent, its failing finances. Throughout the world sociological factors suggest an irreversible trend of population flow from country to towns and from towns to cities. We are in the age in which man is increasingly surrounded by concrete, herded together in vast urban conurbations. In Britain the Church still caters best for the social structures of town and country. The old city churches have lost their appeal and are largely abandoned, while the inner-city areas, often where the need is greatest, are depleted in terms of manpower and finance. The obvious pattern today is that the best maintained churches, in terms of numbers and quality of manpower and financial viability, are in those comparatively "respectable" areas, where most Christians seem to live and where the Church gets its strongest support. Whereas in those less salubrious parts of towns and cities, where the largest number of people are gathered and where social and moral problems are greatest, the Church is comparatively weak in leadership, and often needs heavy subsidisation in order to keep going at all. There are some interesting figures for the Church of England which bear this out. At the moment two-thirds of the clergy of this Church are in parishes with populations of 5,000 or under and over a quarter with populations of under 1,000. When we turn to the laity the picture is even worse. In other words, where the need is greatest, the Church is weakest. Ninety per cent of Christians are evangelising ten per cent of the world, while the remaining ten per cent are trying to reach ninety per cent of the world. Jesus Christ taught a different equation. In the parable of the lost sheep the shepherd left ninety-nine per cent to seek the one per cent that was lost. But what happens when it is the ninety-nine per cent who are lost? The same trends are evident wherever you look in the world; there are many Christian ghettos, and little adventurous moving into difficult and even dangerous fields.

In addition to manpower, financial and deployment inadequacies are structural deficiencies. The churches, generally speaking, are structured for the laissez-faire attitudes of a bygone age. The structures of the Church are largely inadequate to deal with the rapidly changing situations that are arising in many quarters. Church leaders tend to think conservatively, and imagination is at a premium. The watch dogs of ecclesiastical propriety guard the *status quo* and yap loudly and incessantly when anyone steps out of line. Many are dissatisfied with church structures which may have been adequate for the pre-industrial age, but which have failed to adjust to the new trends of an age which should be seen *not* as a threat to the very life of the Church, but as presenting it with unprecedented opportunities, provided the Church can discover a new flexibility to reach society for Christ.

So here is a dismal story of declining manpower, shortage of money, poor deployment of resources and structural inadequacies. But when we have a hard look at the state of the world, this completes the gloomy picture. For as the Church seems to be declining in effectiveness, so it appears the needs of the world are growing in complexity. As the needs are increasing, so the wherewithal to meet those needs is declining at the same time. For one thing the population of the world is growing rapidly, which means more people to reach than ever before. As Cardinal Suenens has put it, "We are sent to everyone without exception. I remember a parish priest saying to me, 'How can I go and visit twenty thousand parishioners? It is impossible.' I answered—well, the command of the Lord is 'Go bring the gospel to every creature.' *The solution must be found; you have to find it* ... you must find ways of acting in full co-responsibility with all the Christians around you so that the gospel is brought to everyone in your parish."[3] As the population of the world grows, the effectiveness of the Church to reach the world should grow also. The present situation has to be reversed. We have to find the answer, for God does not give us commands which cannot be obeyed. A way needs to be found.

But population growth is not the only problem we face. The population of the world is not only growing rapidly, it is also moving more freely and frequently. People do not settle for long in any one place. In the USA one in five families moves every year. The increasing mobility of people poses major problems for effective pastoral and evangelistic measures. The turn-over of the members of our churches is very much more than it used to be, so that it is much more difficult to teach and train, and to weld a team together for effective work and ministry. At the same time our target in evangelism is a moving one. The neighbourhood is constantly changing. As we begin to reach people, so they move off elsewhere and our opportunity is lost. Psychologist Courtney Tall writes of friendships in the future, "The stability based on close relationships with a few people will be ineffective, due to the high mobility, wide interest range, and varying capacity for adaptation and change found among the members of a highly automatic society".[4]

And there is another factor. The new mobility of people not only undermines a sense of security which is important for human well-being, but it also increases tensions. The new technological society, which has followed the industrial society, is one which is creating its own mental and physical problems. It seems that man is more than ever in need of the gospel of Christ, and the care and concern which is so time consuming and which the Church's ministry is so unable to meet. When man's needs have never been greater, the Church seems unable to cope with its own problems, and to be beset with financial and administrative crises, thus rendering it less than ever free to deal with the massive problems of people around it. Alvia Toffler speaks of many people who "cannot cope rationally with change" so they fall into "drug induced lassitude, video-induced stupor, alcoholic haze—when the old vegetate and die in loneliness ..."[5] Between the permissiveness of youth and the loneliness of old age stretch many other corridors of pain along which many have to pass, and which demand help, areas where the gospel of Christ and the power of the Spirit have particular relevance. But where are the resources in the Church today to deal with growing VD, drug dependence, rising crime, loneliness and suicide, and the hundred and one neuroses induced by bad family or community relationships—the underlying fears and hates of generations that have never known the stability of a truly loving relationship?

On top of all this are the plain facts of the alienation of many people from the Church and all that it stands for. The stock of goodwill is rapidly running out. Most people are tired of watching the Church so ineffectively tackling such problems. The minister is an increasingly remote figure, who seems to know little about anything, and who, although he may exude a general benevolence, is much too busy keeping the institution going to have any time for people. Services are either dull and dreary, or so obviously professionally stage-managed to be good entertainment value, but not much else.

The Church is neither loved nor hated. It is ignored by most, and pitied by some. It could hardly have fallen on harder times. Whilst there are moments of domestic euphoria, when some reunion scheme is passed or some leader says something important, most of those involved in church affairs know that they are losing the war. Just as the old wartime communiques about "shortening the line" wore a little thin when repeated so often, and were a euphemistic way of saying "we are retreating on all fronts", so we know that the Church, generally speaking, is failing at a time when it needs to be succeeding. And where is the answer?

It seems a hopeless situation. But in this assessment the state of the churches in relationship to faith itself has not been taken into consideration. There must be few periods when the Church has been so unsure of its faith in God. For some there has been a thorough repudiation of the chief Christian verities. But many others are now unsure, and voices from pulpits are sounding uncertain notes. If many are not yet denying the Christian faith as such, they are not proclaiming it with anything like the convictions of other generations. Faith built on shifting sand like this, cannot last for long.

One thing is certain. New methods cannot hope to succeed unless there is also radical renewal of conviction and spiritual life within the Church. The Church must recover its faith and its message, otherwise we shall simply be moving the pawns around the board, and never getting to grips with the real situations. The solution which has been discovered by the Church of the Redeemer would never have succeeded in terms of methods alone, had there not been at the heart of the renewal a radical change of spiritual life, restoring to men and women their convictions concerning Christ and the power of the Spirit. This would not be the place to set out a suitable confession of faith, and the minimum (or maximum) requirements for such a confession. But it would consist of faith in Jesus Christ as the Son of God and only Lord and Saviour of man, and in the fact that man's salvation was not achieved by human kindness and generosity, but by the "goodness and loving kindness of God our Saviour" who saves us "not because of deeds done by us in righteousness, but in virtue of his own mercy by the washing of regeneration and renewal in the Holy Spirit which He poured out upon us richly through Jesus Christ our Saviour so that we might be justified by His grace and become heirs in hope of eternal life". (Titus 3: 4-7) Commitment to such a faith—and a personal commitment to such a Lord, would seem minimal requirements for that spiritual renewal that the Church should experience. There are still far too many who take such things for granted in our churches; who know nothing of what P. T. Forsyth called "the soul's despair and its breathless gratitude". Added to all this should be the dimension of the Holy Spirit, and the experience of charismatic gifts, which is so much part of the life of the Church of the Redeemer. Our churches need to have the experience of Pentecost, power from God in the person of the Holy Spirit, in whom Jesus said the Church was to be baptised. Without such an experience of the Spirit, the Church in general and each Christian in particular, is bound to be weak and ineffective. We have shown how Graham Pulkingham came back to his church with this power, and the results that followed from it. The gifts of the Spirit—prophesying, healings, working miracles, words of wisdom and knowledge, speaking in tongues and so on, are also important for this renewal. The Church can, and has, existed without them, but when they are not present the Church is that much less effective and Christ-like, and for effective renewal they are vital, particularly if the Church is going to break out of its present serious malaise. Only when the Church recovers its faith in Christ and its experience of pentecostal power can it hope to move the world and transform people. Let the Church acknowledge its bankruptcy, for without these it can do nothing worthwhile. All the money, skill and resources in Christendom, without the blessing of Christ and the effectual working of His power—cannot achieve the goal that God is setting before us. The solution will never be found in mere human forms.

During the last decade we have witnessed the spread of the charismatic movement, sometimes in a spectacular manner, throughout the churches. It has been essentially a renewal in terms of faith and spiritual life. Charismatic gifts have been experienced. Many have found a new faith in Christ and a powerful experience of the Holy Spirit. But, as yet, there has been comparatively little concern to break through in the larger area of tackling the problems which have just been outlined. Certainly a vast new manpower has been recruited for the Kingdom of God, but the dispersal and deployment of this force has been disappointingly ineffective, and most of those involved do not seem to be facing the problems or are even aware of their existence. The movement is robust, but amorphous. Herein lies its greatest strength, and its most prominent weakness. But it does not seem to have come to consider in any depth what new forms of ministry should be developing; how they should relate to existing structures; what "new look" the ministry itself should have; how local churches should be changed in order to deal with the present situation. The major effect so far seems to have been in terms of *individual* piety and spiritual drive, rather than the creation of a new corporate dynamic.

The Church of the Redeemer, Houston, has pioneered a new way of living, and a new style which has all the marks of being something which can be adapted to most situations, and is very likely to channel spiritual renewal in such a way that it can influence the world on the kind of scale necessary for an age such as ours. It has not just "happened". At the back of it are carefully weighed principles of life, which if generally accepted by Christians could bring about that transformation of church life and the Christian style of living which is what so many are looking for. Ideas so far have not been radical enough to change the existing state of affairs and allow the power of God to be released in the Church itself. The Houston way of life is flexible enough to deal with any kind of situation or change of circumstances, so that a church which accepts in a large measure such an outlook, can always keep abreast of the state of affairs pertaining at any given moment. This is crucial for the future, since change is likely to be more rather than less part and parcel of modern life.

There is in fact no shortage of manpower or finances in our churches. But there is a very serious and wasteful deployment of these resources, as we have already seen, both in terms of what these resources are and how they are deployed. Much of the manpower is deployed in wasteful and unnecessary tasks, and there is a shortage of funds to provide salaries for men and women in areas where the need is greatest. *But the Church of the Redeemer has proved that by living together in household communities, much more money, skill and resources are released for ministry in the Church and world.*

The area in which this church lies is a fairly typical "no go" church area, where normally no viable church structure is possible. In Britain such churches are often subsidised by outside funds in order to stay open. They could hardly contribute enough for one ministerial salary, let alone support one assistant and provide accommodation for them and keep the church building going. But this church is now able to support a full-time staff of over thirty men and women, without any financial support from outside. Moreover, there are over forty households, representing around 500 people, attached to the church *and the neighbourhood* and opening their homes and hearts to people in need, so that a large number of people are able to be ministered to personally, and if necessary supported and maintained in a household until such a day as they have recovered. This church sees its role as ministering to the whole needs of people, and all those within its area who want its help.

At the Birmingham Church Leaders Conference in 1972 one of the commissions considered the theme "Man's stewardship of God's world". One of the suggestions made by this commission was for "a personal life style"—"a simplicity of life which is generous towards others and which is content with enough rather than excess". The context of such a "life style" was the world, increasingly polluted and marred by man's greed and excess—a worthy enough motive for such a "personal life style". But there is an even more important and worthy motive, whatever the state of the world, namely that Christians should live a simple life—*for the Kingdom of God's sake*. That they should be prepared to forsake marriage, wealth, privacy, ambitions, honours and promotion, for the sake of Christ and His people. If such an attitude were adopted, then a new and flexible labour force could arise within the church, move into areas where the need was greatest, supplementing and supporting existing ministries. Those involved could be free to stay or leave, as led by the

Spirit and by the collective wisdom of the Church community. Some would work in secular jobs—others would be full-time in the Church. Some would be ordained; some unordained. Most would live together in homes, thus cutting many expenses and costs, as well as other advantages. Such a way of life is not without its snags and difficulties. There is no pathway through life free from such problems. But in this case the advantages far outweigh the problems. Of course, the Church already possesses such resources in its many communities and religious orders. But on the whole these are regarded as exceptional vocations—and inapplicable to the normal church situation. The local church has never been seriously thought of as a possible setting for such a style of life. The Houston way of Christian living is almost without parallel, for in this church many ordinary men and women, who had not made vows as the Franciscans, Dominicans and others do, nevertheless have found a flexible way of life so that their gifts and financial resources can be placed at the full disposal of the Lord and His Body, and on a large enough scale that the major slice of the church's work and ministry is taken up with the worship of God and the redemption of people rather than maintaining structures.

Could this not be the way forward that so many people are seeking? There seems no reason why what has been achieved so successfully in Houston could not happen, with local variations, in any other part of the world. But the Houston way is radical and costly when it comes down to the practical implications; and so it needs examining very closely.

5

Determined to succeed

WHEN GRAHAM MOVED to Houston he was determined to
succeed. He came from an intellectual background and had a
real aversion to anything "enthusiastic". He had kept well
clear of a prayer group that met in his previous parish in
Austin, Texas, and behaved suspiciously like Pentecostals.
But when the Bishop offered him the Church of the
Redeemer, he was prepared to exchange life in a comparatively affluent suburb of a university town for the tough life of
Houston's slums.

Houston's urban development has been typically hap-
hazard. The city bounds have increased twenty times over in
the last fifty years. In the 1950s the blacks began to find
emancipation, and to move out of their ghettos. Eastwood,
where the Church of the Redeemer is situated, was one of the
districts they moved towards. The flight to the suburbs by
the whites began, and what had been a comparatively prosperous area of town, took on a new look. Property became
dilapidated, and the poor blacks and whites moved into the
area where property values plummeted. The area became

increasingly the haunt of vicious elements in Houston's society.

In attempting to analyse why this church succeeded against all the odds, we need to unveil certain principles of church renewal, each of them dependant on the others and demanding a wholehearted response.

One can detect seven of these principles:

Hope
Determination
Brokenness
Power
Losing one's identity
Fellowship
Listening

Hope

Hope is one of the most important words in the New Testament. It is also among the more neglected and misunderstood. For many people it relates only to the supreme Christian hope, the return of Christ to this world. For others it is another word for wishful thinking. So when we say "we hope so", we mean "It would be very nice if it happened, but there is some doubt that it will". Hope does refer to the return of Christ (as in Titus 3 : 7), but the word in the New Testament has a very much fuller use, for much is going to happen before that final return, which is an area of hope for the Christian. The word hope, rightly understood, does not necessarily imply any doubt at all. It is something that has not yet happened, but it will in God's time. It is often linked in the New Testament with faith. But faith is more concerned with the "here and now". Hope lies in the future. But it is no less certain for all that. The two are brought well together in Heb. 11 : 1, "Faith is the substance of things hoped for ..." Faith takes and receives what has been promised or is "hoped for". Like a bulldozer it nibbles away at the soil in front of it. The driver from the vantage-point of his cab can see where he is going and the land which is yet to be reached. It is an *area of hope*. When the bulldozer gets its teeth into it, it becomes an area of faith.

It is good to see more Christians living in the area of faith, claiming and receiving the promises of God. But there still needs to be that ability to see beyond faith, if we are to move in the right direction.

Another word we might use for hope is *vision*. Proverbs tells us that "Where there is no vision, the people perish". We all too easily and frequently wander directionless because we have no vision to see where we are going, no hope to pray for our safe arrival.

A sad commentary on all this is the words of Ernst Bloch, a Marxist philosopher, "The principle of hope that was the genius of early Christianity, a principle by which all reality was understood—is no longer to be found in Christianity, *it has been taken over by the Communists*". Harvey Cox, commenting on this in his book *On not leaving it to the snake*, says "It is the Communists today who look with confidence to the future, while Christians think wistfully of their lost provinces and departed privileges".[6]

Before Graham Pulkingham came to Houston he had a vision given him of what the Church of the Redeemer could be. From the beginning of his time there he travelled hopefully towards its fulfilment. His vocation, to use his own words, became at times "a hideous burden". It was at such times that the vision kept him going and lifted the burden. It was the hope of it that carried him through.

He came to this church believing that he was God's man for the job. At that stage he had all the wrong ideas about how the vision was to be fulfilled. But he was willing to be God's man, through failure and disappointment. The hope never faded, although at times there were some close calls.

The vision he had was of a truly servant church, ministering the life of Christ to the community around it. It was not an indistinct utopian dream—wishful sentimental thinking. It was very concrete and specific. From arriving in the parish every step Graham took seemed to be taking him in the opposite direction to where he thought he should be going. It was all the more important under these circumstances that the vision remained, the hope unimpaired. For there was little wrong with the basic vision, only something radically wrong with the man.

Each church must recover the concept of hope, as it is rightly understood. We need to see where God is wanting to lead His people and what the ultimate objectives are. Each local church should be seen in prospect as a powerful and functioning body of people—the Body of Christ—with a full orbed ministry, each part working properly and truly building itself up in love, as well as offering to the world at large the same compassion and power that Christ showed on earth. To see this, and to hope for it, is not to put it in the vague future, thinking that we shall not see it happen in our day, but to see it coming to pass piecemeal before our very eyes, even if we do have to wait awhile. Many a person gives up hope too easily, often because the hope is not based on a God-given vision.

There are twin dangers facing the Church today, the one is to put everything in the area of hope, often in the vaguest and most impractical terms, which is a convenient way of escaping the uncomfortable demands of a faith which believes in the power of God to change people and circumstances. The other danger is to see only a day at a time. We can only *live* this way, but we are intended to *see* further than the end of our noses. There is a cheap kind of Christianity current today that thrives on instant miracles, immediate success and a cheap and undemanding gospel. Patience in such a setting is a totally unnecessary virtue.

Christians need bi-focal spectacles—a part to focus on near objects, so that we have faith to act in the day-to-day circumstances of life; and the other kind of lens, to deal with distant objects, so that we can see beyond the present, and be as sure of the distant scene as of that which is immediately present.

Determination

Graham was also very determined in his attitude to his work. He still is, but the natural determination of a resourceful person has been transformed by divine grace. There is serenity and dignity about his new determination.

It is important to link hope and determination together. Determination without hope only leads to endless nervous frustration, which can in the end bring one to the point of breakdown. One becomes so much involved in the problems, that one becomes part of the problems oneself, instead of part of the answer. It is like trying to hack your way through a dense jungle *without a compass*. One will only go round and round in circles, getting more and more exhausted. On the other hand, hope without determination is like a becalmed sailing vessel. Even with the finest navigational instruments and the skills of the most competent navigator, it will get nowhere until the wind begins to blow again, and one gets under way once more.

Christians need to come to terms with the fact that God's will is not going to be done on earth without "blood, toil and sweat". There should be that complete surrender to the will of God, and determination to see it come to pass, *whatever the cost or the price*. The few in the Church of the Redeemer in Houston, who were to lay this sound foundation, were determined, whatever the cost, to see their vision come to pass. And because it had been a divine vision, not a human illusion, or a taunting mirage, it did come true. They gave up everything, laying down their lives for each other, so that God might be free to create a community of love that would be the spear-head of God's intervention in the world around them. They were determined to succeed, and because God was with them, and they were moving in obedience to Him, the momentum was not their own, but His, and success was assured.

Many talents were laid at the feet of the church, to be used to God's glory. Graham himself had been wonderfully prepared for this venture. His theological training was part of the preparation. So was the musical instruction he had received. In the navy he learned the art of leadership. As a hospital chaplain he discovered the various areas of human need, and the psychological basis of man, as well as some ways of meeting that need. He was to be joined by a doctor and a lawyer, both highly trained and competent in their professions. But following Christ and building the Body of Christ were more worthy objects for which their talents were to be used than professional adroitness for its own sake. They were first followers of Christ, and brothers and sisters in the Lord, and only secondly theologians, doctors, lawyers and psychologists. It was Graham's determination which brought him to the crucial points which revolutionised his ministry. If he had been a starry-eyed idealist, looking for some utopian situation in the dim and distant future, rationalising the failures of the present in the light of a totally impractical future, he would have got nowhere. He knew the difference between success and failure. He was a realist. He knew failure in all its humiliation—and his determination brought him inevitably to brokenness. It was there that a new faith was born which was to bring him, this time with a divinely directed determination, to the success which had been his hope in the first place.

Those who lack determination, who are half-hearted and give up easily when the battle becomes hard, should not be disciples of Christ. The man who puts his hand to the plough and looks back is not fit for the kingdom of heaven. The person who is looking to God to provide an easy and painless pathway to success, will always be disappointed.

Brokenness

Graham had to taste some of the bitter fruits of failure before God could make much use of him. Graham, like others today, had to learn that intellectual training in itself and all the talents and resourcefulness to go with it, can be useless to God. Indeed they can so often get in the way and become a substitute for the real work of God in human life. So long as a person trusts in these, all the determination in the world, and even real vision with it, will not bring success. If God Himself is left out of account, then there is no essential difference between a man of God and an inspired and determined humanist.

Strong and resourceful people usually need to be humbled and broken before they can be of use to God. Graham had been brought into a kind of situation in which there was no hope whatsoever apart from God.

Graham's pride was hurt. He was tempted to self-pity. Had he not after all given up an attractive appointment to minister in a truly terrible situation? He was reluctant to admit failure, although it stared him in the face. He turned increasingly to tranquillisers and other drugs to still the storm inside himself, as he still fought on with all the determination he could muster to turn dismal failure into success. But it did no good. The harder he tried, the more his frustrations grew. There was only one outlet left for him, so he broke down and wept. Not once or twice—not for a day or a night, but for weeks on end. It may not be a wholesome spectacle to see a man weeping his heart out. Modern man is too proud for that. Uncontrollable sobbing broke out from the depths of Graham's soul. But here is a sight which God looks upon with great delight. It is a sign that a man has come to the end of the road, and is ready for God to take over. Graham's hope was failing—his determination was sagging. His whole world was breaking up around him—and the cry was beginning to taunt him—"Where is *now* thy God?" In his own words, "I shook my fist at the God of this dilemma and demanded to know the cause of my failure". You can hear the frustration in the voice of Peter, the big fisherman "We have toiled all night and caught nothing". Graham in his pit of self-despair would never have guessed that he was about to turn the corner, and before long, like Peter, he was going to catch a shoal of fish.

Power

The story has already been told how Graham found his way to New York, and walked and wept round the streets with David Wilkerson. The apostle Peter came along the same road from total failure, when he denied his Lord three times, weeping bitterly when he realised what he had done, to the day of Pentecost when the power of God came upon him, and he stood before a huge crowd and preached that Jesus Christ was Lord. Graham, too, passed through a valley of misery, to his personal Pentecost, when he was baptised in the Spirit. It is not enough to know human weakness, and to experience brokenness. If we do not recognise this, then bitter experience may have to teach it to us. For we have also to know the power of the living God. "You shall receive power," Jesus promised His defeated and broken disciples— *"when the Holy Spirit is come upon you ..."* Graham's story is being repeated all over the world. In the contemporary charismatic movement many of God's people are re-discovering for themselves the power to which Jesus Christ referred. All over the world Christians are being baptised in the power of the Spirit. To Graham this was not an end in itself, but the means to the end, of building up the Body of Christ, and extending the range of the Kingdom of God. It was not the end of the road to recovery, but the beginning of a new way of life, lived no longer in human strength, but dependant on the resources of God. He came back to Houston to find the place was the same, but *he* had himself been changed, and the results began to speak for themselves.

The charismatic movement has been the means of directing many back to the truth that Pentecost is meant to be the contemporary experience of every member of the Body of Christ, and that without the promised power of God, the Body of Christ will be incapable of providing for its own needs, let alone the needs of the wider world. For springs and streams of water are not enough, the world needs *rivers*, and these flow neither from our heads or our lips, but our innermost beings.

Later on Graham received the gift of speaking in tongues. But he never regarded that as the secret, or the key to the power which he had received. It was a further gift which the Lord gave him when he asked for it. The word soon got around in Houston that Graham was baptised in the Spirit, but the work at the Church of the Redeemer was never allowed to be influenced by what was going on outside it. Graham never became an apostle of a new movement. The power he had received, as he saw it, was to be channelled through the Body of Christ, which in this case was the Church of the Redeemer, to the needs of the world. What had happened was crucial to all that was to follow. Without his experience of the Spirit Graham would never have seen God at work in his own life, let alone that of others. God had allowed him to be broken, that he might be filled, purified from selfish ambitions and proud self-confidence so that men would say, "God has done this thing". But having said all this, the truth remains that the experience on its own could have been frittered away on trivialities, or mis-directed into a vague amorphous movement rather than concentrated into the vital task of building up the local community, so that it might approximate in every dimension to the God-ordained pattern. The power was not to be squandered on lesser matters but directed wholly towards the church becoming in reality the Body of Christ on earth.

Losing identity

Graham came back to Houston after his experience with a strong sense of call. He had never, even in his darkest moments, completely lost that sense of destiny. Now he had a new confidence. The hope was going to be fulfilled. The events immediately following his return only served to underline his convictions. There was a touch of the invincible about everything he did. But it was at this point that he had to learn the most important secret of all. Some of us, when we begin to walk by faith, have to go through the same trial. Abraham did when he took his son, "born of faith", his most important and precious possession, and truly a gift of God, and was told to sacrifice that gift on Mount Moriah. Graham now had a ministry which he had longed for. Now things were happening before his very eyes which he had never seen before. God, as it were, said to him, "Graham, I want you now to sacrifice your ministry to me".

This is a subtle, but most important key, for it can unlock doors into completely new experiences of church life. It is, however, all too often overlooked. In the first flush, and also when the euphoria first passes away, those who have tasted for the first time the joys of new life in the power of the Spirit, hug their gifts to themselves, selfishly indulging themselves in the blessings which have come to them. But Graham calmly took the next step also, in his own words—"I was prepared to lose my identity". Wisely he saw that he could not possibly minister, even if he had all the gifts, to all the needs of the Church of the Redeemer. He could have made it alone, for he was a gifted person. But he chose to surrender to others, and to share his new ministry, in partnership with whoever would go along with him. And once a man is willing to do this, there will be no shortage of those willing to come with him. The test of effective leadership is what happens when the leader is absent. A church ought to be able to continue to grow and thrive, even when the leader has been removed. When a leader is absent from a church, the difference ought not to be noticed; this is how it has turned out at the Church of the Redeemer. The rapid and dramatic expansion has not been the result of one man's brilliant leadership. It has been a co-operative effort from the start, with gifted lay leadership, and a church full of people ready and willing to lead or be led, to minister or be ministered unto, whether the person concerned is officially "ordained" or not.

One thing is certain, a one man ministry was never

intended to be the pattern for the church, and has been proved a hopeless failure wherever it is practised, yet it seems to be still in essence the norm rather than the exception in most churches. The answer lies in a man's willingness to "die". Delegation is not enough. There is not one law for the "minister" and another for everyone else. If the gap between minister and people is to be closed, then it should begin with the minister's willingness to "die". Jesus said, "Unless a grain of wheat falls into the ground *and dies*, it remains *alone*. But if it dies, it bears much fruit".[7] How simple—and yet how hard for us to practise! The blossoming of such a widespread and profound ministry in the Church of the Redeemer was only possible when Graham was prepared to share his ministry on an equal with others, and to let them contribute their gifts, and encourage them to develop their own roles alongside his own.

From this time onwards the story of the Church of the Redeemer is not about one man and his ministry, but the story of a group that was totally yielded to God. Cardinal Suhard, the spiritual father of the French worker-priest movement, once said that it is not the task of Christians to advocate a programme or ideology. Rather their task is to create a mystery that cannot be explained by any human system of thinking and can finally only be understood as the grace of God. The "mystery" of the Houston story has only one explanation—the grace of God. Graham was prepared to lose his identity for the sake of all. This was the essence of the real mystery of how the Church of the Redeemer came alive.

Fellowship

The most immediate and obvious impression that any visitor to this church has, is of a closely related family of people, who are as totally committed to one another as they are to their Lord. They are often together. They share life freely. There are no strings attached, no areas of reservation, no place for a "no go" area of privacy. But it is important to realise that this fellowship which has developed over several years does not exist for its own sake. It is not a super religious club. It has not been allowed to become unhealthily introverted. It exists for ministry. Its members are there to serve, not primarily to be served.

It is true that there are some weaker members whose contribution appears to be minimal. Some of these are "stretcher cases" and will possibly remain so for the rest of their lives. The fellowship serves them, and supports them in a truly Christian spirit. "The poor you always have with you," was how Graham described it, quoting our Lord's words. But a strong and outward looking body of people will always be able to support some of these people, although many others have been brought to the church on "stretchers", who were later seen "walking and leaping and praising God". The Redeemer Church does not look anything like a cosy convalescent home for spiritual cripples.

The foundations that were so surely and deeply laid in the first few years of this church's recovery, included this basic principle, *that the main purpose of sharing a community life, is not primarily for its own sake, although experience has proved that the most healthy Christian development towards wholeness of life comes in community living, nor because it happens to be becoming fashionable even in secular society; but fundamentally because only in this total life of sharing can the full potentials of ministry develop in the local church.* Only, for instance, when the comparatively wealthy share sacrificially, will the funds be available to support those who are gifted in certain areas of ministry, but who cannot devote their time to it because of the need to work for their living. Only when those who are gifted in household affairs, in the practical day to day art of living, use their gifts communally, will those with other gifts be free from burdensome chores to give their time and talents to those who need them most. Community living is undoubtedly liberating, even if it has problems of its own, for it delivers people from some of the wasteful efforts at living, while at the same time being financially less demanding.

The fact that this church was prepared to lie hidden for several years is of the utmost importance. For it was in their discoveries in the area of community living that their future strength was ultimately to lie. Had they not been patient and worked hard at the establishing of deep and sound personal relationships, it is doubtful whether the later outreach would have been possible. Certainly the main strength of this church lies in these personal relationships. They have pioneered a way through the morass that many churches find themselves now in, which is leading some to doubt whether a church can ever again in any practical sense be a gathered community of people.

Listening

Last but by no means least, this community of Christians learned from the start how to listen and how to hear and know the will of God, so that they were then sufficiently in serious business with God to obey Him. We have for the most part lost the art of listening. "The word of the Lord was rare in those days" is descriptive of our day as much as it was of the day of the prophet Samuel. There is no shortage of *words*. Never have there been so many books written about God, nor so many sermons and discussions. But at the same time it is a comparatively rare thing if anyone ever really hears God speaking clearly and unmistakably.

But at Houston they found themselves listening and hearing, and sometimes receiving some strange and peculiar directives. It is not that they heard audible voices. But deep in their own hearts, and as a collective body of people, they were convinced that God was telling them to do things, sometimes quite out of keeping with logic and reason.

Some people, when referring to "hearing God speak", think solely in terms of the Bible. Therefore, to hear God speak today, you have to read the Bible. It is as simple as that. "When you read the Bible, God speaks to you; when you pray, you speak to God", one was often told. But this is an unfortunate over-simplification. It has led some to proof textualising themselves through life, summarily dismissing what God may be saying to them through someone else, and claiming that God's word (i.e. the Bible) has spoken to them already, whereas in actual fact they may be self-deceived, claiming divine authority for what is their own thinking. The Bible can and does speak to us. But God's word, relevant, real and personal comes to us in other ways too.

In the case of the small nucleus of Christians in the Church of the Redeemer, they were hearing God speaking to them long before they knew their Bibles very well. Most of them had only a rudimentary knowledge of the Bible. Graham Pulkingham himself confessed that virtually the only book he studied in seminary was the Gospel of St. John, and he was ordained with only the haziest of ideas about the Old Testament. This is not, of course, to disparage knowledge of the Bible. It is only to say that it is possible to be so saturated with the Bible and biblical texts that one may not hear God speaking. We can think that the Bible itself is God to us, whereas in fact it is the mouthpiece of the one who is the Word of God—Jesus Christ Himself.

"No-one knew the scripture ahead of time," says Dr. Bob Eckert of the Church of the Redeemer. He meant that they would often turn up a Bible passage, realising then that God had already spoken to them about that particular matter. God does not have to wait until we know the Bible before He can speak to us.

So from the earliest moments they knew the difference between the letter "that kills" and the Spirit "who gives life". They knew too that God usually speaks to and through groups. In Proverbs we are told "in the abundance of counsellors, there is safety".[8] They were not simply to wait for the brightest ones to get the lead from God. Certainly not to depend on the Rector for every lead, and then simply to rubber stamp all that he said. Sometimes the weakest members were used by the Holy Spirit to sow the seed idea, which was to blossom later in a new direction for the fellowship to follow.

But the nucleus of God's people in the church there, did not fall headlong into the opposite error, that of ignoring the Bible. On the contrary they gave themselves to a diligent study of it. Graham himself set aside more time than he had ever done before to study and to try to understand it. One of the more conspicuous features of the church as it is today is its concentration on Bible teaching, with study groups meeting every day of the week. They will instantly reject anything which is contrary to the express teaching of the Bible.

The members of this church are Bible-loving believers, who seem to have escaped from the trap of "Bible worship". The Bible has its important place, but the Lord has the supreme and unique place as the One who speaks to and directs His people. And they have become sensitive as a church to seeking for and discovering the will of God, even if it does mean waiting a long time for it to be revealed.

Here then are seven vital principles which have helped to hold the whole thing together, and enabled the Church to survive the shocks that every work of God suffers to a greater or lesser extent. And notice how closely they relate to each other. Without hope one hardly gets started. Without determination one easily gives up. Without human brokenness and divine power, one quickly breaks down. Without "losing one's identity", the power cannot spread through the church, and fellowship cannot develop freely. Without the ability to listen to and hear God's directives, the whole enterprise loses its way. The crisis facing the Church at the present time will not be overcome easily. Success will only be assured when we learn to give ourselves to God—and one another. and receive fully all that God has to give us.

6

Free to serve

The correct philosophy of church administration is set forth by
two general principles:
    (1) talk constantly about the democratic nature of the church's
organisational structure.
    (2) so organise your parish that all really important decisions
are made only by you.

Charles Merrill Smith, *How to become a Bishop without being
religious*[9]

IT IS OBVIOUS for all to see that the Church is facing a leadership crisis, and no amount of "papering over" can hide it.
According to Hans Kung there is clear evidence that "the
crisis is approaching disaster point".[10] During the past 25
years the number of ministers and priests in the United States
dropped from 250,000 to 200,000, a fall of twenty per cent.
In the same period, according to *Church around the World
news digest*,[11] mental health personnel (psychiatrists, psychologists etc.) jumped from 14,000 to 100,000. The editor
comments, "Is the psychologist taking the place of the pastor?"
It is a question worth pondering. At the very moment society
is having to enlarge its ranks of professionally trained personnel to cope with mounting mental sickness, the Church
is having to close its ranks owing to the decline in recruitment
for the ministry. Bishop Dean, a former executive officer of
the Anglican Communion, when he retired from office in
1969 morbidly gave the institutional church ten years. "If our

church dies in its present form," he said, "it will die from
self-strangulation by its own prosperity, *we possess all things*
—that's why we have nothing." There are many who believe
that unless something radical happens soon, there will be a
complete collapse of effective leadership in churches throughout the Western world. The growing number of early retire-
ments, and in some tragic cases early deaths, of Christian
leaders, speaks eloquently enough of the stresses and strains
so many are having to face as burdens increase and manpower
and finances diminish.

It is important, therefore, to understand how the Church
of the Redeemer, Houston, has in the same period developed
such powerful and comprehensive leadership, and discovered
at the same time the secret of mobilising the full resources of
the laity to serve the Church and the world.

But there may be some who would question whether it is
appropriate to use this church as a possible model for other
churches to imitate. Being an American church, some might
think that it had access to funds which would not normally
be available to the average church. As a matter of fact,
churches in the United States are not normally subsidised as
many are in Britain by central funds, nor supported by the
State as most continental churches are. They have to stand
on their own feet, or close. And the Church of the Redeemer,
throughout this period of change and growth, has been viable,
and has never received financial aid from outside. The reason
why they have been able to pay their way is not to be found
in the giving of a few wealthy benefactors, but in the general
attitude and principles of church life which could be appli-
cable in any other church situation.

Others might draw attention to the fact that the leadership
has been unusually able and inspired; that Graham Pulkinghams are rare, and that the success of the church has been
largely due to his personality and gifted leadership, a factor
you cannot expect in the majority of churches. Leadership is
a crucial factor, and it is true that Graham Pulkingham
does possess a number of gifts which are not usually found

in the same person. It is also true that Graham's leadership
has been a vital aspect in the success of the Church of the
Redeemer. But we have already observed that one of the
most important keys to success at the church has been the
ability Graham has had to "lose his identity" and share his
ministry with others, and so not allow his personality to
dominate. Since 1969 he has been away from the parish so
much that the personality factor no longer counts. The
church goes on without him. His influence was strongest at
the beginning, but he so managed things that he virtually
did himself out of a job. There is no reason at all why men of
lesser gifts, provided they are prepared to share the leadership with others, cannot see similar results in the same time
as it has taken for the Church of the Redeemer to develop
its powerful ministry.

Others might say, "This has happened in America, and in
a certain kind of area. It could not work in other settings or
countries." However, when we consider the work of the
Church today one thing is certain, it is in the inner-city areas
that it is most obviously failing. Normally it is here where
the Church is weakest. The fact that the Church of the
Redeemer has succeeded in such an area should encourage
one to believe that similar success could be achieved anywhere else. There are bound to be non-recurring cultural
factors which would make the Church of the Redeemer differ
from churches in other countries, or even other cities in the
United States. Different sociological backgrounds would need
to be taken into consideration. Obviously one is not suggesting
that this church and the way it has developed should be an
exact model for every other church to imitate. Each church
should be led by the Holy Spirit and there are bound to be
differences of approach. But there are still basic and vital
biblical principles which are incarnated in Houston, and
which can and should be applied in most church situations
today. The detailed applications may be different in varying
situations, but the principles remain constant throughout.
One is arguing for a radical new approach which can provide

the church with a much more varied, dedicated and flexible ministry, which can be adjusted to any and every situation. It would, therefore, be a false argument to say that the Church of the Redeemer was so exceptionally provided for in terms of finance and leadership that it should not be taken seriously as a model for other churches.

Let us look at these principles more closely. The first is fairly obvious and universally accepted, namely that the Church consists of all the people of God, and all the people of God are called to minister in the Church. Hans Kung has defined it, "The Church is the entire *community* of those who believe in Christ, in which *all* may look upon themselves as the people of God, the body of Christ and the temple of the Spirit ... the specific factor is not that one enjoys an 'office' in the Church (and the kind of 'office' it is); what matters is that one is a 'believer' pure and simple: that is, a person who believes, listens, serves, loves and hopes".[12] There is no need to spend longer on this basic point, since it is so well established. But in practice many do still think that only a few people are called to minister in the Church; and the laity are still to a large extent the Church's "frozen assets". To use the same terminology, we need the full "liquidity" of these assets.

But obviously there are varieties of ministries in the Body of Christ. This is a fact which Paul is at pains to stress. "There are varieties of gifts (*charismata*) ... service (*diakonia*) ... working (*energemata*)" (1 Cor. 12:4) he writes. Although all Christians are called to serve, their service or ministry will vary considerably. Each member (like the human body) has a different function, but each person functions "for the common good" (1 Cor. 12:7). They should complement rather than compete with one another. Again, although there is universal acceptance of this principle, in practice the whole subject is bedevilled in the Church today by false and artificial distinctions made between the ordained and unordained. In Houston this distinction is not made so sharply. While the church accepts the order and disciplines of the Episcopal

Church, and its ministry has never been questioned by the authorities, the criterion whereby the proper functioning of ministries is determined, is made on the basis of what they call "anointing". And this needs explanation.

An "anointed" ministry, put simply, means that the gifts and abilities have so obviously been bestowed on a certain person by the Holy Spirit, that this is self-evident to the Church at large. In the Church of the Redeemer they trust the Holy Spirit to provide all the necessary ministries so that the church is able to function properly; they therefore look out for the persons who obviously have the supernatural "anointing" of the Spirit for each particular function. The question whether that person has been "ordained" is not of primary importance. Nor is his training or preparation. The major question is whether God has gifted him, and whether he can function properly and fulfil that particular role in the Body of Christ.

But it is important to see that such "anointings" as they are called, are regarded as being to the church rather than the individual. The Holy Spirit's concern is with the whole Body of Christ rather than individuals as such. An example of this principle can be seen in an incident in a meeting at the church. Graham Pulkingham was present at the start of the meeting, and clearly was anointed to lead the meeting. Then he was called out suddenly and unexpectedly. While he was away from the meeting the anointing shifted consciously and clearly to Jerry Barker, one of the lay leaders. But the moment Graham returned, the anointing did also. Another ordained priest who was present at the time did not receive the anointing, but Jerry Barker, a layman, did.

It might be important here to try to clear up some mis-understanding regarding the differences between "ordained" and "unordained" or lay ministries. This is leaving aside the domestic regulations of the Episcopal Church which rule that only episcopally ordained priests can celebrate the Services of Holy Communion, or be called to the office of Vicar or Rector. There are at least four major differences commonly (but mistakenly) held, between the ordained clergy and the laity. The first is that the ordained minister has more authority, and some would say spiritual power, by virtue of his office. The second is that he is more fully trained. The third is that his office is more permanent in the sense of being a life-long vocation and also in terms of staying in one place for a reasonable length of time and with, generally speaking, a fairly clearly defined function in the Church. The fourth is that he is more fully committed to service in the Church, he is a full-time professional in the religious field.

Now these distinctions are far too arbitrarily set, and would be totally unacceptable in the Church of the Redeemer. As we have already seen, whatever official status an ordained man may have, a layman might in certain circumstances (as in the meeting described earlier) have an anointing and, therefore, an authority, which an ordained person present might not possess. And certainly it is untrue to say that ordained ministers necessarily have more spiritual power than the lay person. They sometimes do, and they sometimes don't. The determining factor is the gift of God, and the degree to which the power has been appropriated rather than who the person happens to be or what "office" he holds. Then, so far as training is concerned, it is increasingly obvious that ordained ministers are not necessarily better educated, or trained for ministry in the Body of Christ than lay people. It is true they may possess a certain clerical know-how and theological knowledge which others do not have. But in terms of leadership, knowledge of people, counselling techniques and understanding of the Bible, lay people are sometimes better prepared and able to minister than professionally trained ministers.

A major difference, however, is concerned with whether the ministry is permanent or not. No-one seriously questions the layman's right to move from church to church when the location of his job changes, or for other reasons, such as promotion at work or greater wealth. The layman, too, tends to be a jack-of-all-trades in the Church, seldom settling down very permanently to anything in particular. But such an attitude needs to be challenged, and in the Church of the Redeemer a layman's ministry is as much a matter for concern as an ordained person's. Since the layman is called to minister in the Body of Christ as well as the ordained minister, why should his role be conceived of as of a semi-permanent nature? As we have already mentioned, it is generally assumed that a clergyman is fully committed to service in the Church. But why should such an assumption be made? In certain circumstances a minister may be part-time (just as Paul manufactured tents while carrying on an apostolic ministry); in other cases a layman may be full-time in the service of the Church (as some are in the Church of the Redeemer). The important factor is not whether one is ordained or not, but what one's ministry is in the Body of Christ, and lay people should act with as great a sense of responsibility as the ordained towards that ministry. It is often forgotten that Jesus was a layman, for He held no "office" in the religious set-up of His day. Yet for three years He was "full-time" when called upon to leave the comparative security of the carpenter's trade in Nazereth for the uncertainties of an itinerant ministry. He also called others to forsake their professions, in some cases temporarily, in others permanently, without giving them the security of a particular "office".

In the Church of the Redeemer there are over thirty full-time workers. A few ordained. One is a Methodist minister working in the church with the Bishop's permission. But the majority are not "ordained". Some travel, others remain in Houston. Some are single, some married. Some are on small salaries, the rest receive nothing, but are supported by the rest of the church fellowship.

The thinking behind this approach to ministry has been deeply influenced by the teaching of Paul in Ephesians, chapter 4. In Houston they talk often about "the five-fold ministry", meaning apostles, prophets, evangelists, pastors and teachers (although they usually class pastors and teachers together). They talk about it as being "the gift to the church",

and "the anointed authority of the church". Those called to
these ministries are regarded *jointly* as the leadership of the
church. When I asked Dr. Bob Eckert who took charge of
things when Graham Pulkingham was away, he was at pains
to point out to me that several people did, not one supreme
deputy. When Graham was there, although officially Rector of
the church, he shared this authority with others who had been
called and anointed to lead the church with him.

They see the ministry of apostles as concerned with ini-
tiating, establishing and renewing churches and other areas of
Christian endeavour. Dr. Bob Eckert's visit to Mexico (see
chapter 10) is a good example of apostolic action. Bill Farra's
six month visit in 1971 to All Saints, Auckland, New Zealand
is another example of apostolic work. The prophetic gift or
the ministry of the prophet is to give direction and guidance
to the work of the ministry. Every new direction which the
Church of the Redeemer has taken was initiated through
prophecy. Having regard to the imaginative approach in so
many areas of ministry and the success which has attended it,
this speaks much for the importance of this ministry in the
church. With regard to the sheer mechanics of this prophetic
ministry, guidance did not come usually through some prophetic utterance ("thus saith the Lord, thou shalt go to
Mexico on October 14"), although there were occasions, for
instance before they set up the highly successful coffee house
work known as "the Way in" when visions were given by the
Holy Spirit which were later fully authenticated by the events
that followed. Normally the prophetic ministry is exercised
when the leaders talk and share together about certain
matters. Gradually they discovered that certain people had
an uncanny gift for seeing the heart of the matter, and
understanding and declaring the will of God. It is interesting
that one of the titles of the prophet in the Old Testament
is "seer".

The ministry of evangelism is a fairly obvious, though
much neglected one. The term "evangelist" usually refers to
someone who travels round from area to area holding cam-

paigns or missions. It is seldom thought of in terms of the local church. However, in the Church of the Redeemer, the evangelistic ministry is seen in terms of persons who have obviously been given power by the Holy Spirit and gifts for that task, working closely with the other ministries. This church regards the evangelist as having a rather wider role than "preaching the gospel", although this is included. The evangelist is one who brings God's word and blessings to individuals, whether they are Christians or not.

Pastors and teachers are those who shepherd the flock, feeding and caring for them. They lead the worship and spend much time teaching and counselling. They are also responsible for disciplining and correcting the church, so that it's life and ministry may be truly wholesome. In the Church of the Redeemer, in addition to the Sunday services, there is a daily Eucharist at noon, and daily prayer and Bible study meetings in addition to the ministry of the Word in each household community. There is plenty of scope for pastoring and teaching. They regard this pastoring and teaching as "a community of ministers". The pastor speaks for the community of ministers, not vice versa. In other words, there is not one "boss", but several leaders, who meet regularly and who share and agree together. So when the pastor speaks on any issue, he expresses the united mind of several people.

The five-fold ministry does not, of course, exhaust the spheres of ministry in the church, or the gifts which are manifested. There is the important ministry of music, for example. Then there are administrative gifts, and the equivalent of what the New Testament calls "help". There is also the ministry of giving financial assistance where it is needed.

It should be stressed again that there is no way of "graduating" to a particular ministry. You cannot learn how to be an apostle or a prophet. You either possess the anointing or you do not; and no man can give that anointing to anyone or secure it for himself. It is divinely bestowed and divinely maintained. God can also remove it. Normally it is self-evident, the Body of Christ recognises the ministry because it can see that the person has the God-given anointing; and the church recognises the ministry and accepts it gratefully.

All the ministries thrive on love. Paul in Ephesians 4 speaks of bodily growth that "upbuilds itself in love" (verse 16). He begs them to lead a life worthy of the calling to which they had been called "with all lowliness and meekness, with patience, forbearing one another in love" (verse 2). The Rev. Jeff Schiffmayer, present pastor of the Church of the Redeemer, writes "the first lesson we had to learn as a body is still the most important one; the effectiveness of our ministry depends on the fervency of our love for each other. Thus the parish and in particular the individual homes of the parish have become the training ground for discipleship and ministry."

If the ministries of the Spirit are to develop and come forth, and be used for building up the Body of Christ, no one individual should be allowed to dominate the church. If such people arise in one church it is possible that they are intended to be a gift to the whole Church (and, therefore, to be set free to travel) rather than to dominate one local church and so stultify the rest of the ministry in that church. Such a person is probably called to be an apostle. Individualism has been the bane of the churches, and one of the main reasons why they have not developed in the freedom of the Spirit.

What one sees at Houston is the coming alive of the total church or community to minister to itself and to the world in love and freedom. "The Church," writes Hans Kung, "is the total community which, announcing the gospel ... awakens faith in Jesus Christ, evokes commitment in His Spirit, makes the Church present in the world in the form of everyday Christian witness and promotes the cause of Jesus Christ."[13]

However, there are some basic hindrances which can prevent such a vision being fulfilled. There needs to be a sacrificial giving of oneself to Jesus and to one's brethren if they are to be removed. The success of Houston has largely come about because many of the members have seen clearly what these hindrances are, and have been so sure and committed to what they knew to be the prior claim on their lives, that they have been prepared to sacrifice anything and everything to be completely obedient to that vision. The vision was to see a church free to minister fully and completely to itself and the world around it. Many people have seen this vision and hoped for it to be fulfilled. But not many have seen the hindrances that prevent this coming to pass, and even fewer have found the way through. Houston saw these hindrances, counted the cost and paid the price to remove them.

7

Drop everything

It makes no difference who you are,
It makes no difference where you are going to:
When Jesus calls to you,
Drop everything and go.
        Diane Davis, *Songs of Fellowship*
        (published by the Church of the Redeemer)[14]

WE HAVE ALL seen commuter traffic pouring into our cities
in the morning rush hour. Bumper to bumper, the cars edge
their way forward until they reach their destination and spill
into overcrowded parking lots or beside greedy parking meters
that devour coins hungrily. One cannot but ponder the sheer
waste of time, money and nervous energy which this morning
(and evening) farce represents, quite apart from the exhaust
gases which pollute our overcrowded cities and the occasional
smashes which kill and maim thousands of people every year.
Most of these cars have one or at the most two occupants—
a frustrated driver and perhaps one nervous passenger. How
much more sensible to halve the number of cars, and get
each car to take two other passengers. Or better still clear
the streets of all but cars on essential journeys, and improve
the capacity and scope of the public commuter services. The
serious problem of our overcrowded roads is one of many
inevitable results of the new affluence which has made the
car an essential commodity. At the same time soaring rents
and house prices spotlight another dilemma of modern

society which not only requires that one owns and runs a car but also a house.

Switch the scene from rush hour traffic to the more tranquil setting of Sunday worship in church. Here too there are frustrations mentioned earlier, serious financial problems, shortage of staff and an increasing inability to cope with the demands of the ministry. There just is not the time or the wherewithal to fulfil the tasks to which the church is committed. And yet in actual fact most churches possess hidden but so far untapped financial resources. The same is true of manpower and the time that can be given to the essential ministry which is the worship and glory of God and well-being of people, rather than the maintenance of an institution. It is simply, like the morning rush hour scene, that we have not been taught to share our resources and to be involved *together* in the business of living, and so releasing these resources which are otherwise wasted by sheer duplication.

When it comes down to it the church's ministry consists of people, men and women, who have time to give to it, financial support for it, energy to carry it out, and a degree of flexibility so that they can keep at it without being moved about by circumstances other than those dictated by the Spirit of God. People, time, money, energy and freedom. But in most churches the majority of members are so involved in the business of living that they have little time and insufficient money to spare for the work of the Kingdom of God. Mammon has a prior claim over God. So much energy, and unfortunately nervous as well as physical, goes into daily life that there is little left over for ministry in the Church and in the world. The professional ministry can be just as much affected, particularly in Britain where salaries are still in many cases barely sufficient to keep a man and his family. In other words there is a great deal of wasted duplication of possessions and time which could be channelled into the work of God, if the local church could begin to share rather than duplicate its resources. To maintain an effective ministry, particularly in areas like the inner-city, where there is very little commitment to or involvement in church life, there should also be a much greater degree of freedom for Christians to remain in one area if necessary for many years in order to minister freely in the local Body of Christ. Such people should not feel obliged to move because the firm moves or wants to move them or because of family circumstances. We shall discuss the place of the family in the next chapter. If by remaining a person loses their job or suffers financial loss, this should be the concern of the local church, which should, if necessary, be able to support that person and the family if there is one, so that the person's ministry can continue. The tragedy is that many churches, particularly in the comparatively depressed sections of our cities, have a constant and chronic manpower deficiency because their lay leaders, who are often few and overworked anyway, are at the mercy of every kind of whim and fancy of the world, which can suddenly and irrevocably whisk them off to another part of the country and so deprive the local church of an essential ministry. In our inner-city areas the migratory tendencies of the population are well known. But if the church is to function properly it is essential that these tendencies are resisted by those who are members of the local Body of Christ.

Let us summarise by saying that in the normal circumstances of today the average church can call on only a fraction of its manpower and material resources because so many of its people are expending time, money and energy on the business of living in the increasingly demanding circumstances of modern life with all its accompanying strains and tensions. The church's potential labour force is seldom available in the right place and for sufficient length of time to make it effective, owing to the pressures of modern work patterns. The inevitable result is that the more gifted members tend to drift into the more affluent areas which become over staffed with leaders, while the less affluent and more needy areas are denuded of Christian workers and have constantly to cope with irregular and temporary manpower. In other words, instead of the Kingdom of God "calling the tune"—the world does. A side-effect, of course, is that more strain comes on the professional ministry, which becomes more and more taken up with comparative trivialities, and the Church instead of being galvanised into action becomes increasingly institutionalised, taken up with preserving itself rather than serving God and the needs of the world.

At this point we need to turn to the New Testament to see if it has anything to say about such a situation. It is of great significance that we find the most relevant passages in the writing of Luke—his gospel and the Acts of the Apostles. Of the four authors of the gospels, Luke is the one who emphasises Jesus' concern to draw people to Himself and to meet their human needs. In the Acts of the Apostles his primary concern is to show how the Church functioned, particularly in apostolic outreach, and how its resources were mobilised for this task. In Luke's choice of material he is constantly referring to Christ's compassion for the outcasts of society, and the demands that He made upon those who aspired to be His disciples. In no other gospel is the cost of Christian discipleship more explicit than in Luke's. We can see how relevant this is to our subject. Luke draws attention to a sea of human need, to a society divided against itself by greed, suspicion and prejudice, and to a "Church" so absorbed in petty shibboleths as to be incapable of meeting those needs, and in some cases being actually responsible for them. Into this area of need moves the Son of God—healing, forgiving, loving, caring. He calls a band of men and women around Him, to be with Him for fellowship and to share in this work of compassion. He himself has sacrificed everything to be free to carry on this work. And He expects nothing less from all those who aspire to follow Him. To the person who said "I will follow you wherever you go," Jesus replies, "Foxes have holes, and birds of the air have nests; but the son of man has nowhere to lay his head." (Luke 9: 58) And when He called on others to follow Him, they proffered prior claims, one "to bury his father" another to "say farewell to those at home". Jesus indicates He cannot accept disciples on such terms. Such an attitude renders that person "unfit for the Kingdom of God". Later on Jesus tells the parable about the man who issued an invitation to a banquet.[15] But they all made excuses. Again it is concern for property and possessions on the one hand and family or married life on the other which hinders them from coming. One has recently bought a field, another has bought some oxen and the other has got married. The man is angry, and sends his servant out again, no longer to the property owners and those who have the security of wealth and family, but significantly to the poor and maimed and blind and lame, in other words the under-privileged members of society. Our Lord ends this parable with the solemn words "none of those men shall taste my banquet".

What our Lord is saying in these passages is that nothing should stand in the way of the person who wants to share in the ministry of Christ. The claims of home and family, posses-sions and work, are always secondary to that of following Christ.

Again and again Jesus asserts the primacy of ministry and service over that of acquiring possessions and wealth. When someone asks Him to intervene in a dispute over a will, no doubt concerning property and money, Jesus refuses to be-come involved. Instead He warns the person who asked Him, "Take heed, and beware of all covetousness; for a man's life does not consist in the abundance of his possessions."[16] He goes on to tell a story which gets us to the heart of the whole matter. It is about a rich man who, instead of distributing his harvest surplus to meet the needs of others, decided to "store it up", or in other words "capitalise it", thus also insuring a higher market price and, therefore, greater profits, even though others may have been starving around him. But that night Death visited him, thus depriving him at one stroke of everything he had acquired. "So is he," Jesus says, "who lays up treasure for himself and is not rich towards God." In St. Matthew's gospel Jesus puts it even more bluntly. "Do not lay up for yourselves treasures on earth, where moth and rust (or as we would say inflation) consume, and where thieves break in and steal (income tax, capital gains tax and death duties); but lay up for yourselves treasures in heaven, where neither moth nor rust consumes and where thieves do not break in and steal. For where your treasure is, there will your heart be also."[17] Such words cannot be explained in any other way than that Jesus called upon His disciples to forsake money making and the acquiring of assets such as property and capital unless they could be put to use as resources for the Kingdom of God.

Of course money will always be needed, as well as property and possessions, if one is to live at all. But what Jesus is emphasising is that the pursuit of these for their own sake, unrelated to purposes of ministry, is out of keeping with the principles and objects of the Kingdom of God. These are hard sayings indeed to those who live in a capitalist society, where the virtues of acquiring the security and status that wealth provides are stressed openly and plainly. But when one sees how much the mobilisation and deployment of the Church's manpower resources are let and hindered by the pressures involved in acquiring such securities, one should be more than ever convinced that Jesus was right, and discipleship for all Christians involves putting Him, and the ministry that He calls us to, before all other considerations.

In the narrative that follows the so-called parable of the rich fool, Jesus tells His listeners not to be anxious about providing for the bare necessities of life, food and clothing. In the famous passage (paralleled in the sermon on the mount) Jesus tells them to consider both the ravens and the lilies of the field.[18] Do not "be of anxious mind", He says, "for all the nations of the world seek these things; and your Father knows that you need them. Instead, seek His Kingdom, and these things shall be yours as well." Yet in practice how much nervous energy and how many worries and anxieties are involved in the whole matter of living! How much time and effort, instead of being employed in the service of the Body of Christ and the world in its massive need, is instead devoted to maintaining a living. Jesus goes on to say, "Sell your possessions, and give alms; provide yourselves with purses that do not grow old, with a treasure in the heavens that does not fail, where no thief approaches and no moth destroys, for where your treasure is, there will your heart be also." Jesus calls His people to dispense with everything that is unnecessary or surplus to maintaining a simple life, all that may hinder or get in the way of our fulfilling our ministry in the Body of Christ. And if this means selling everything, then we should do it. If it means moving from a salubrious district to a shabby and neglected area of a city, then we should do that. If it means refusing promotion and even losing our job to remain where we are, we should gladly accept such a sacrifice, knowing that the Kingdom of God primarily is not meat and drink but "righteousness and peace and joy in the Holy Spirit".[19] Our possessions and the acquiring of status, wealth or position should never come before obedience to our Lord in the fellowship of His people.

In the Lucan beatitudes there are some notable differences from those recorded by Matthew in the sermon on the mount. Jesus says "blessed are you poor" (where Matthew has "poor in spirit"), and "blessed are you that hunger now" (where Matthew has the spiritual concept of hunger and thirst after righteousness).[20] Luke also adds a series of parallel woes, the first of which is "woe to you that are rich, for you have received your consolation; woe to you that are full now, for you shall hunger".[21] It is not without significance that we hear so much more in our churches of the Matthean beatitudes, which are spiritualised, than the more nitty-gritty beatitudes of Luke's gospel. Is it that the Christian Church finds the exaltation of poverty and hunger embarrassing and prefers the spiritual equivalents?

When we turn from Luke's first volume to his second, we find he implies from his prologue that he is writing about the continuing activity of Christ in the Church. "In the first book, O Theophilus I have dealt with all that Jesus *began* to do and teach", implying that in the second he tells about all that Jesus *continued* to do and teach. It is not, therefore, surprising that we find the principles He laid down for discipleship accepted by the earliest converts without demur or argument, though in one sad case there was deceit which ended disastrously for a husband and wife. In order that the Church might be free to minister to the world and sustain its own life, it immediately, from the day of Pentecost onwards, shared its resources in a simple form of community life. There was no obligation or rules involved, no vows were taken as is clear from what Peter said to Ananias, "While it (the property) remained unsold, did it not remain your own? And after it was sold was it not at your own disposal?"[22] The rule of love was the over-riding principle. On the day of Pentecost, Jesus gave the Church all the divine resources necessary to enable it to sustain its life and fulfil its mission. He poured out the Holy Spirit upon them. The Church in sheer gratitude and willing response made available to God all its resources, for "All who believed were together and had all things in common; and they sold their possessions and goods and distributed them to all, as any had need."[23]

The important thing to notice about this sharing of assets and resources is that it had a two-fold thrust. On the one hand it was an act of human compassion to meet human need, not a sentimental form of idealism. And secondly it was done in the context of worship, witness and service, and no doubt was a major contribution to the flexibility and effectiveness of the early Church's resources particularly in terms of manpower and deployment. It was done that Christians might be free from anxieties related to poverty on the one hand and the management of property on the other. Whereas in the gospel of Luke the man in Jesus' parable says "I have bought a field ... have me excused," the early Christians said, "I have sold a field ... so I'm completely free to do what you say and go where you direct."

The day of Pentecost is not the only reference to such benevolence in the Acts of the Apostles. Nor can it be cited as a rash action, a rush of blood to the brain which was never repeated in the light of maturer reflections. We are told some time later that "The company of those who believed were of one heart and soul and no one said that any of the things which he possessed was his own, but they had everything in common ... there was not a needy person among them, for as many as were possessors of lands or houses sold them, and brought the proceeds of what was sold and laid it at the apostles' feet—and distribution was made to each as any had need."[24] No wonder in the same context Luke records "Great grace was upon them all."

On the whole the modern church has treated these references condescendingly. Indeed the phrase "the Jerusalem experiment" has been commonly employed, and the generally accepted view is that these were rather extreme measures adopted in good faith, but later dropped when the Church was more mature. In other words, they were the product of a kind of adolescent enthusiasm. But later wiser and more balanced counsels prevailed. But such an interpretation does scant justice to the texts, nor does it do justice to what lay behind these acts of generosity. When these acts were committed there was no sense whatever that they were "experimenting". It was, according to Luke's account, a spontaneous act of love, not a carefully calculated experiment. And, as we have already seen, it was repeated later when the Church had time for maturer reflections. Moreover devastating judgment fell on the luckless Ananias and Sapphira when they sought to do the same thing, only holding back some of the proceeds whilst pretending to give all. It would seem unlikely, if the Church later regarded it as an experimental action, that Luke would have given such unqualified prominence to this aspect of the Church's life and action. But Luke, far from regarding it as a passing phase in the Church's life, an extravaganza which was unique and unrepeatable, saw it as a totally consistent follow-through of all that Jesus began to do and to teach before His death and resurrection.

When later on the Christians in Jerusalem fell on hard times, and famines reduced them to penury, we see the Macedonian Christians providing for them out of their own means, and thus themselves benefiting as Paul explains to them in 2 Corinthians. He tells them that their abundance "at the present time should supply their want, so that their abundance may supply your want, that there may be equality" (8: 14) One has heard it said that if only the Jerusalem Christians had been more sensible and not realised their capital so radically, they would not have needed this help later on. This is a rather hard-headed businessman's approach to the matter. Self-sufficiency is not one of the fruits of the Spirit. To be so generous that you become dependent on others is an incitement to their generosity in return, and it is in these practical ways that the Church is welded together.

But this way of life did not end with the New Testament. The same attitude was adopted by the Church consistently throughout the first three centuries. Father René Carpentier, S.J., and a team of young Jesuits at Louvain have done a ten year study on all the Christian texts of the first centuries. Carpentier concludes, "The *koinonia* (Christian community involving total sharing) formed part of the ordinary catechesis of all the faithful. In the documents we are dealing with, it was the normal practice and not the exception."[25] Father Max Delespesse writes in the same vein, "The teaching and practice of a community of goods is so closely linked to the ordinary Christian life that when the texts don't mention it, it is because the matter is so evident and well-known."[26] He goes on to give textual support for this assertion. He shows that it was never a matter of obligation. "Some gave everything they owned to the Church, but this was not obligatory ... what does oblige everyone and applies to everything is the need to share. Certainly this community of goods will appear in diverse forms according to circumstances and it will vary according to the degree of faith and the hope of Christians, but it will always appear as the indispensable sign of divine love and brotherhood in Christ."[27] Delespesse ends with the question, "Are we dealing with a new social order?" And he answers, "Yes."

It was the post-Constantine Church which must be blamed for the change which took place in the attitude of Christians towards their possessions. Harvey Cox has pointed out that after Constantine, poverty belonged to the monastic system. It was the monopoly of a dedicated religious élite, not for the vast majority of believers. Poverty was no longer virtuous. From now onwards virtue consisted in *giving* to the poor.[28]

But it is most important that we understand why the early Christians behaved as they did. The basis of their action was altruistic rather than idealistic, practical rather than theoretical. It was also motivated by the desire to be free to minister fully in the Body of Christ and to the world at large, as well as a generous concern for the material needs of the brotherhood. But most local churches will not need to give too much attention to material needs amongst its members. Yet there is a pressing need that there should be greater disengagement with worldly cares and the sheer sweat of modern living. For some this will mean a total giving up of possessions and earning capacity. For the majority it could mean a partial disengagement. For others it might mean a total engagement in the world, but a re-channelling of the resources gained for the benefit of the Church as a whole. At all events the overriding consideration in all this should be obedience to Christ and the ministry He has given in the Body of Christ. At the same time it needs to be said that it is contrary to true love for any Christian to hold on to possessions when at the same time another person has needs which otherwise would not be met. As John has put it, "But if anyone has the world's goods and sees his brother in need, yet closes his heart against him, how does God's love abide in him? Little children, let us not love in word or speech but in deed and in truth."[29]

Finally, let us look and see how the Church of the Redeemer has worked all this out in practice, and how the hindrances of possessions and finances have been converted into resources for the Kingdom of God. The first thing that needs to be said is that no-one in the church fellowship is under any obligation. As Peter put it to Ananias, their possessions and money are entirely at their own disposal. They can keep them, or give them away. The overriding principle is love. If we love our Lord and His people, and if He gives us His compassion for the world, then all that we have and all that is ours will be laid at His feet.

> "Love so amazing, so divine,
>   Demands my life, my soul, my all."

is how Isaac Watts puts it in his famous hymn.

If the Church is to be free to minister, and if that ministry, is to be flexible to meet every human need and situation, then Christians should freely and joyfully be prepared to surrender everything to that end. And this is what has happened in Houston.

Let us see how various members of the Redeemer fellowship approach all this. For instance, there are some who have good jobs which command fairly high salaries. They have not been called by God to sell up everything and throw in their jobs. However, they are anxious that their whole life should be part of the total ministry of the Body of Christ. So they have taken seriously what Paul says in Romans 12:8, "he who contributes, in liberality" or the King James rendering, "he that giveth let him do it with simplicity." They do not interpret this to mean that they are to live up to their means, with a large home, several cars, a country cottage, a boat and all the other concomitants of modern gracious living. Albeit, giving a generous percentage of their income to the church, and witnessing faithfully to the upper echelons of society that they move amongst; at the same time attending church regularly, although in their case they might well live some distance away in the affluent suburbs and drive there on Sundays and the occasional weekday. Not at all! To contribute "with simplicity" means to them, selling up their unnecessarily large home, dispensing with their other surplus commodities, living a simple life in the depressed section of

Houston's community close to the Redeemer Church, so that they can give a large part of their income to the work of God in that church. Thus they contribute practically to its total life, since their ministry of giving helps to support the ministry of several other people, who, therefore, are set free from the task of "bread winning" in order to concentrate on the ministry to which they have been called. Thus financial resources freely made available and not squandered in unnecessary opulence are channelled into the total ministry of the church and enable another member or two of the Body to function, which they would not otherwise be able to do.

There are others in the fellowship who are professionally trained to a high level of competence such as Dr. Bob Eckert, a medical practitioner, or Jerry Barker, a qualified attorney. To begin with, after selling up their prosperous practices and moving from the affluent suburbs, they were able to live in the vicinity of the church and set up medical and legal practices nearby. But they have also felt free at any time to leave the practice of medicine and law respectively to travel in an apostolic ministry or to serve in any other capacity in the Redeemer Church; all for the total good of the whole community, rather than simply the whim and fancy of the individual. This is a good example of the flexibility that this church has discovered, so that there are manpower resources available and free to meet the changing demands of the church and the world, especially in the new patterns of life which are part of an ever changing urban neighbourhood.

There are others too with practical skills who have made their talents available, some on a part-time basis, others in a full-time capacity, knowing that the Redeemer community will support their ministry if they are really called of God, and that there will be resources available to sustain it, even if the style of life is simple and without frills.

Then there have been disturbed people who have come to the church for help, or been contacted by church members. To begin with perhaps they have been unable to contribute anything. They have been casualties in the battle of life. But as they have begun to respond to the love of Christ in the setting of a live fellowship, so they have been able to do more and more. Some are extremely talented people, whose gifts have been either undeveloped or rendered useless because of the nature of their illness. Still others have gifts they are unaware of. As they find release in Christ's love and through His Spirit, so these gifts are discovered, and used to the glory of God. These kind of people, the maimed or lame members of society, have found not only healing in the Redeemer Church, but a place to minister and to put to good use their various gifts, some artistic, some practical, some spiritual.

As the fellowship has grown, and especially as they have developed the household communities, which we shall be examining later, so they have launched various practical schemes to enable the Body of Christ to function freely. Our Lord, when He spoke about our not being anxious, referred especially to food and clothing, the most basic requirements of life. The Church of the Redeemer has a large and well-stocked clothes store in the basement of the church building. The clothes are not cast-offs, nor is it intended primarily for vagrants or hobos. The clothes are sometimes given, sometimes bought from bankrupt sales, and sometimes through economic bulk-buying. They are free and include most basic items. They may not be the most exclusive fashion lines, but they do provide clothes for a fellowship of people who are not primarily concerned with smartness for its own sake, but who want to live as economically as possible.

Once a week a truck from the church runs down to the nearest wholesale food market and fills up with fresh fruit and vegetables. The goods are then displayed on the floor of the church hall, and members of the household communities come each week to collect their share of what has been bought, at a fraction of what they would have cost had they been shopping in the supermarkets.

During our second visit to Houston we were impressed with this aspect of the life of the church. The food eaten in the households was simple fare compared with what is normally served in American homes. But it was wholesome, and the methods employed of bulk buying at knock-down prices must save thousands of dollars, thus releasing more resources for the ministry of the church. The result is that a large number of people are able to work full-time because of this simple way of living—and because their basic needs are met in this communal fashion. We can see even more clearly that there are great economies in *time* as well as money in living together. By sharing in household chores and other aspects of home life, many more people are set free to serve in the fellowship of the church. There are so many ways of saving when Christians share fully and freely.

Jerry Barker explained this aspect of their life together in an article in the *New Covenant* magazine.

"It soon became obvious that the needs we were faced with would take lots of resources and so we began to cut expenses for things we had been accustomed to. We stopped buying new cars and new televisions and things of that sort. We didn't even think of them. We started driving our cars until they literally fell apart and then we'd buy a used car or something like that to replace it. We began to turn in some of our insurance policies so that they would not be such a financial drain on us. We found such a security in our relationship with the Lord that it was no longer important to have security for the future ... we never have had any rule about it, or felt this was a necessary part of the Christian life. It was just a matter of using the money we had available most effectively, particularly in supporting so many extra people. We learned to live very economically. We quit eating steaks and expensive roasts and things like that and we began to eat simple fare ... we'd often eat things that people would bring us—a box of groceries or a sack of rice..."[30]

When on Sunday one looks round the average congregation it is not unlike the Monday morning commuter traffic referred to earlier. As a body of God's people supposedly united in ministering the life of Christ to the world, we are so often travelling to heaven, like rush-hour commuters, in our little boxes, more or less isolated from each other. We mostly live separately and run our cars separately. At Sunday lunch-time there are hundreds of meals prepared (each one separately) from food which has been shopped for separately. Hours of time and hundreds of pounds are being wasted every week. At the same time the Church frets about the shortage of manpower and financial resources. How foolish and how wasteful we can be! Is it because we know little about what it is really to love and care for one another, and share the journey of life together that we may more freely and generously share the life of Christ with the world around us?

8

A new way of living

A new way of living
A way of forgiving
West Side Story

WE HAVE ALREADY seen how uncompromising the claims of Christ are upon those who choose to follow Him through life. When the guests were invited to the great banquet, property and possessions, according to Jesus' parable, were used as an excuse for not coming. One man had just bought some land and the other some oxen. But another person, who had been invited said "I have married a wife," and made this an excuse for not attending. So also, when Jesus called someone else, he made the excuse "Lord let me first go and bury my father." Jesus replied, "Leave the dead to bury their own dead; but as for you go and proclaim the Kingdom of God."[31] Jesus is here unequivocally asserting that the Kingdom of God has a prior claim over all human relationships, and that neither marriage nor family should come before it.

It is interesting, therefore, that we find in these two passages in Luke's gospel that the main hindrances to following Jesus Christ occur when possessions and property on the one hand, and marriage and family on the other are given priority over God's call. Having dealt with the matter of possessions we must now turn to that of the family.

It is indisputable that family ties and the whole area of sex and marriage can be a serious hindrance to the Kingdom of God. On the whole people are getting married much younger, so the energies of youth are often absorbed in the whole business of adjusting to the demands of the marriage relationship. Married couples are much less flexible when it comes to Christian service than those who are single. When children are born they absorb more time, and parenthood adds further restrictions on freedom to serve the Lord where and when He wants. And so the most fruitful years of our life can be taken up with the problems of living and caring for a family. So there is little time or energy left for the Kingdom of God. Then, when the children are grown up and married and have young families of their own, they are often involved in caring for ageing parents. We finish up being old ourselves and sometimes being a burden to our own children. So the process goes on. We are married and so do not have time to come to the banquet. We have a dependent father, and must first see him safely into the grave before we can follow Christ wholeheartedly.

We see the matter even more starkly when we notice the wastage caused by Christians who marry unbelievers; families that have to live in certain areas for the sake of the children, particularly from the angle of education; missionaries who have to return to their homeland because of the children's education or to nurse sick and ageing parents; Christian organisations that cannot afford to pay a married man's salary and that cannot get single men for love or money; missionary societies that have a surfeit of single women, and very few single men, and that find taking on married couples a hazardous undertaking, knowing that the health risk is greater and the chances of their completing any reasonable length of service less than that of single people, who can go into areas where married people with families cannot. One can begin to understand why Paul wrote, "I wish that all were as I myself am [i.e. single]."[32]

To add to all this, we are living in extremely bad times in the whole area of marriage and the family, and Christians are far from being exempt from the tensions and strains created by these modern problems. Over many years there has been a progressive breakdown of family life. It shows itself most starkly in the growing divorce rate. In Britain, between 1960 and 1970 the annual rate increased from 23,400 to 57,400, that is about two and a half times. In the United States it is as high as 1 in 4. In some parts of California it has reached seventy per cent of marriages contracted. It is nearly as bad in most of the Western world, and this does not take into account the marriages that survive but are a mockery of what they should be. Christian marriages too are failing and in the United States divorce amongst such people is a growing factor. In Britain divorce is still largely taboo amongst Christians, but there has been a sharp deterioration in the stability of marriages between Christians in recent years.

Of course divorcees have themselves been the victims of broken or frustrated home life. And so the vicious circle continues from generation to generation. Because of the failure of parents to relate satisfactorily to each other we now have what we call "the generation gap". The insecurity and frustrations involved by so many marriage failures means that husband and wife have increasingly been incapable of relating satisfactorily to their children, and so children grow up alienated from them, and often lonely because of the smaller size of the average nuclear family. Cornell University psychologist Urie Bronfenbrenner quotes a cab driver he met in Washington, DC who turned out to be a shoemaker who had a second job in order to earn money to buy his children a tape recorder and other expensive gifts for Christmas. He won't, therefore, be able to see them for six weeks or so. As a parent he thinks that a new tape recorder is more valuable to his children than he is. Parents tend also to attempt to insulate their children from the hard side of life. The same psychiatrist comments, "This notion that children need to be protected and should never see anyone in pain, or old, or smelling bad, is a false notion. How can anyone appreciate joy if he doesn't know what sadness is?"[33]

And so the downward pathway gets steeper and steeper. We have as a result of all this the sight of the modern generation resorting to drugs, permissive sex, and delinquency. Every year in the United States about half a million teenagers run away from home. Growing VD and pregnancies among unmarried girls and abortions is one pointer to the failure of young people to cope with sexual relationships, and adds further to the sum of human misery which stretches for a growing number of people from birth to death. But it would be unfair to see sexual freedom as the prerogative of the young. Casual sexual relations are more and more common amongst the middle-aged, who are often quite as permissive as their younger counterparts.

But few are kidding themselves that all is well. On the contrary, all kinds of radical remedies are being suggested for the present state of affairs. "America's families are in trouble—trouble so deep and pervasive as to threaten the future of our nation," declared a major report to a White House Conference on Children.[33] Some are advocating the ending of the classic family structure. A growing number of people are not bothering to get married. Women's Lib. blames the family for women's present ills, and resents the role that the Creator has given to women as child-bearers and mothers. Sweden's educational system has been deliberately changed to eliminate the differences in the assumed "sex roles." Schoolboys do needlework and study home making, while the girls take courses in repairing cars and manual training. The Swedish Prime Minister Olof Palme has said, "Nobody should be forced into predetermined roles on account of sex."

One needs to look a little closer at our present ills in order to see if there is any answer. It is necessary for us to do this before we turn to examine the teaching of Jesus concerning the relationship of the family to the Kingdom of God. Then, when we look at what has happened practically in the Church of the Redeemer, we shall see that, however controversial at first sight their attitude to the family might be, it is more in keeping with the teaching of Christ than much current Christian thinking, and as a result brings more benefit to the family, and increases rather than diminishes its effectiveness and general well-being.

There are, it appears, four major reasons for the present malaise in the modern family. The first is that society as a whole has become obsessive and permissive to the point of neurosis about sex itself. So in June 1970 *Time* magazine could assert dogmatically, "In the permissive post-Christian world, the idea of seduction as sin is definitely dated." It has reached a point where there is now a significant shift in guilt. There used to be a general and unhealthy sense of guilt about sex itself. Today there is much more a sense of guilt about impotence, and a sense of shame if one is not strongly motivated in a sexual direction. The Dallas psychiatrist David Hubbard has written a book called *The skyjacker; his flights of fancy*,[34] in which he outlines his studies in the psychological make-up of skyjackers. He has found that most of them have failed in their sex lives. On the whole they have not been strong masculine supermen, but failures at life and love. Guilt-ridden by their failures they have resorted to the glamour of hijacking airliners to compensate for their inadequacies. Society today expects and assumes that every person wants and needs sex, and so through advertising and other means of communication, particularly films and TV, the normal person is viewed as the sexually active. The sex drive is regarded as normative, and should usually be indulged freely, legally or illegally. It follows from such a viewpoint that those who do not have it are "queers" in some way or other. Since for Christians marriage is the only permissible area for sexual experience, it means that most Christians seek to be married, and those who do not get married are regarded as either sexually deficient or it is assumed, mainly in the case of women, that they have never had the chance to do so.

But Jesus is judgment itself against such evil suggestions. He never married, and yet is the true Man, the most normal person who has ever lived on this planet. One has used the word "evil" deliberately. Those who today brain-wash society with their sex obsessions are guilty of causing miseries and frustrations to thousands of people. This is one of the principal causes of marriage disharmony, often forcing people into relationships which ultimately prove unsatisfactory. But we cannot blame everything on this aspect.

The second reason for our troubles is the modern attitude to marriage itself. For a growing number of people it has become a form of escapism. Unfulfilled and unhappy people often look to it as an answer to their problems. Instead of which they pool them. Incapable before marriage of forming satisfactory relationships (often because of the failure of their parents), they find themselves equally incapable as the dimension of sexual love is added. "For many," says Graham Pulkingham, "marriage has become the last desperate hope for a dependable relationship. It then becomes a kind of hiding place for people and is presented as the ideal love relationship. In most cases marriage doesn't measure up to these expectations. It becomes a sad knot of periodic pleasure which holds things together, a possessive relationship which produces jealousy, exclusiveness, and hostile and destructive tensions ... it appears as the only option, the last, desperate hope of finding meaningful personal relationships in life ..."[35] Marriage can be a very selfish relationship, both in terms of the children (the generation gap) and the larger Christian community. It can so often be seen in terms of two people forming an exclusive relationship which enables them to get through life without really having to face themselves, which they would have to do in the context of the larger Christian community. This attitude to marriage is comparatively modern. The older family structures were much more inclusive in character, open-ended not only to other members of the family, aunts, uncles, cousins etc., who would probably live near at hand and often visit for lengthy periods, but also to the neighbourhood, so that there would be a constant stream of visitors flowing in and out. It is all part of one of the most dangerous and harmful trends in our society, the increasing splitting up into smaller and more isolated units, and the dying out of any real sense of community.

A third reason for our troubles has been the modern attitude to the family. In 1970 U Thant, then Secretary-General of the United Nations, was photographed prostrating himself, as Burmese youth are taught, at the feet of his eighty-seven-year-old mother before saying goodbye to her. "A son," so the report went, "is never too old or too important to kowtow to his mother." Ancestor worship is, of course, part of the Eastern way of life, particularly in Confucianism. But it is by no means absent in the Western world, even if it is not quite so explicit. "Kowtowing" to mum or dad can be a very serious matter. Whereas on the one hand there has been the collapse of family life in many quarters until it has become almost meaningless, on the other there has been much idolising of it, with possessiveness by parents of their children, and the children themselves continuing to be in a dependent position long into adulthood. Some have been crippled by neglect, others by being unnaturally bound to either parent. One of the most perspicuous portraits of the possessive parent is found in C. S. Lewis' classic *The Four Loves*. Her name is Mrs. Fidget. It was said that she "lived for her family, and it was not untrue ... She was always making things too; being in her own estimation ... an excellent dressmaker and a great knitter. And of course, unless you were a heartless brute, you had to wear the things." Her epitaph is a sad one, "The Vicar says Mrs. Fidget is now at rest. Let us hope she is. What's quite certain is that her family are." C. S. Lewis goes on shrewdly to say, "We feed children in order that they may soon be able to feed themselves; we teach them in order that they may soon not need our teaching ... we must aim at making ourselves superfluous. The hour when we can say 'they need me no longer' should be our reward."[36]

Neurotic sexuality, selfish marriages, possessive parents, are all soil from which sprout the perversions which blight so many people's lives. Homosexuality and lesbianism are perhaps the two most important deviations whose origins, most would agree, go back to unstable and irregular family life. To this one should add the growing drug taking and promiscuous behaviour of young people, whose lives are haunted by the bickerings and quarrels in family life, the sheer strain of trying to live together in reasonable harmony. The data of doom supports this with the lurid statistics of juvenile delinquency, broken homes, suicide, VD, and divorce. "No society has ever survived after its family life deteriorated," warns Dr. Paul Popenoe, founder of the American Institute of Family Relations. "In the last days," Paul warned Timothy, "men will be lovers of self, lovers of money, proud, arrogant, abusive, disobedient to their parents, ungrateful, unholy..."[37] Graham Pulkingham writes, "I think it is becoming increasingly clear that the institution of marriage in our society is failing in almost every respect. The growing number of divorces and multiple marriages, the rejection of family life by a growing number of young people, and the general unhappiness and unresolved tensions in many 'good' marriages all bear witness to this."[35]

A fourth reason for our present troubles is the break-down of all semblances of community in our society. In the lust for economic expansion, the well-being of community life has been largely forgotten. The former Dean of St. Paul's Cathedral, London, Dr. Matthews, has written in his autobiography about his home-town of Camberwell, an inner-city area on London's South Bank, "When I was a boy it was a community, now it is a dormitory."[38] Many attempts are being made to remedy this basic need, few more radical than the kibbutz in Israel. Faced with the urgency of building a new society in the dangerous situation that has always faced the new state of Israel since its formation, young Israelis reared their children in the kibbutz by removing children when four years old from their mothers, allowing them to grow up in "peer groups". Children almost without exception turn out so well that the possibility arises that the breast feeding and mother dependence creed isn't true after all. Kibbutzniks form no deep attachments to individuals and have no use for privacy. All strong emotions are centred on the group and thus group love, loyalty and unity of action apparently persist throughout life.

One's major criticism of such a practice would be that the new social orientation of the individual is achieved but that something very important is lost in the process, namely the distinctive personality of each person and their ability to form deep relationships with other people. What has come about in Houston, by the grace of God, is an approach which, following the pattern of Jesus' teaching, maintains the basic structure of the nuclear family, whilst at the same time opening it up so that it is no longer exclusive, but can truly minister to the spiritual and social needs of others.

To sum up. We see that many people today are deprived both within family life and in the larger areas of society of a stable community. They find it increasingly difficult to form good relationships, and they pass on their own fears and guilts to others. People are being driven more and more in upon themselves, putting up a variety of façades behind which they hide, afraid to face people and to share life at a deep level. The results are tragic. There is a "survival of the fittest". But the majority, the weakest, succumb to various neuroses, or in extreme cases to serious psychotic illnesses, living out a miserable existence, forced to rub shoulders with others, and yet less and less able to relate satisfactorily to them. Becoming lonelier and lonelier, they crave for marriage as the antidote, only finding it at best a mild palliative, at worst the final straw. This may seem an unduly jaundiced view of the situation. But society as a whole is beginning to recognise that more and more people are today victims of what has become known as "stress". It is interesting that the *Sunday Times*, when it did a series of articles on the subject of stress in 1972, referred to, "certain familiar situations—the conflicts of adolescence, *the false expectations of marriage*, the uncertainties of middle age".

But even more tragic than this is the fact that being a Christian sometimes does not seem to make that much difference. Our churches contain strong people who are able to hide their problems successfully and get through partly by sheer will-power and partly by bluff, and weak people, who can be a constant source of concern to the rest of the church, and who continue to display their neurotic symptoms and are the despair of all who try to help them. But the plain unvarnished truth of the matter is that churches can so easily be holy clubs, not communities. They can be launching pads for evangelistic outreach, not a homely caring group of people, "a family", which deserves to have new spiritual children to nurture, or which is capable of fulfilling this role anyway. Or they can be "mass stations" for the regular infusion of grace to face the cruel world. What a distortion of what it really ought to be!

When we turn to the gospels and see what Jesus had to say about sex, marriage and the family we find that He neither endorses the permissiveness of our age, which would ultimately destroy the family, nor the commonly held view of the family, which many Christians adhere to, which isolates and insulates it over against the rest of society and the Church. He would have us neither reject nor idolise the family relationship. The overriding consideration, as we shall see, is the Kingdom of God. Jesus taught that marriage was a temporary relationship for this life only—teaching which the marriage service endorses with its "till death us do part". For Jesus said that "In the resurrection they neither marry nor are given in marriage, but are like angels in heaven."[39] In other words, there is no sex in heaven and no absolute relationships. No wonder when the crowd heard it, they were astonished at His teaching.

It is important too to see that both Christ Himself and the Apostle Paul recommended celibacy, neither giving it a higher nor lower place than marriage. When Jesus had stated

His uncompromising attitude to divorce, the disciples in effect responded with, "it's safer and better not to get married at all."[40] Jesus did not then leap to the defence of marriage and recommend it highly to everyone. What He did say was that marriage is not for everyone, it is given to some. But there are others who cannot marry, and others still whom God does not intend to get married "for the sake of the Kingdom of heaven". Jesus finished these remarks with the words "He who is able to receive this, let him receive it." It is clear that many then, as well as today, would have found it very difficult to accept such teaching. Then as now marriage would have been regarded as the norm, and all those who were unmarried would have been treated as abnormal and peculiar. But Jesus teaches that God calls some to marriage and some to celibacy. It is interesting that today the only suggested solution for the population explosion is birth control. It has never been suggested that more people should be unmarried. At the back of such a view is that normal men and women have to experience sex otherwise they would suffer intolerable frustrations. When man makes sex into a god, it is inevitable that such thinking should prevail. Most Christians (apart from Roman Catholics and Anglo-Catholics) have never been seriously faced with the possibility of God's call to celibacy. To be a single person is viewed by most as a life sentence in loneliness. But if the whole vista of community were to be opened up it could be seen quite differently, and the prospect of sharing life with several others would banish altogether the thought of loneliness. In any case marriage for some has not been the answer to the problems of loneliness.

The apostle Paul wanted all men to be as he was (i.e. single). "I wish that all were as I myself am," he wrote in 1 Corinthians 7: 7. But he recognised that there were different gifts, "each has his own special gift from God, one of one kind and one of another." There is a *charisma* of marriage and there is a *charisma* of celibacy. *Both* are gifts of God.[41] The thinking behind Paul is the same as that of Jesus, that the Kingdom of God is the most important consideration. Paul was so burdened with concern to fulfil the call of God to evangelise the world, knowing that single people are much more free to do such work, that he wanted everyone to be as he was—a single person. C. S. Lewis, commenting on Paul's teaching here refers to "the multiple distractions of domesticity": Lewis goes on, "It is marriage itself, not the marriage bed, that will be likely to hinder us from waiting uninterruptedly on God. And surely Paul is right ... the gnat-like cloud of petty anxieties and decisions about the conduct of the next hour have interfered with my prayers more often than any passion or appetite whatever."[42] But the hindrance is not only on the level of our relationship to God, it is also on that of our relationship to others in the Body of Christ. The Christian family can so easily become a selfish closed shop, for ever involved in itself and having little or no time for anyone else.

We must turn from the marriage relationship itself to that between parents and children. Here too we find a consistent pattern of teaching by our Lord. Again we see that the Kingdom of God is the overriding consideration. It is significant that Matthew tells us that when Christ called James and John "immediately they left the boat (possessions) and their father (family) and followed him."[43] Later in the same gospel Jesus said, "Do not think that I have come to bring peace on earth; I have not come to bring peace, but a sword. For I have come to set a man against his father, and a daughter against her mother, and a daughter-in-law against her mother-in-law; and a man's foes shall be those of his own household. He who loves father or mother more than me is not worthy of me; and he who loves son or daughter more than me is not worthy of me; and he who does not take his cross and follow me is not worthy of me. He who finds his life will lose it, and he who loses his life for my sake will find it."[44] Or even more striking in Luke's gospel "If anyone comes to me and does not hate his own father and mother and wife and children and brothers and sisters, yes, and even his own life, he cannot be my disciple."[45] In these passages the relationship between Christ and His people is regarded as greater than that of any other human relationship. The teaching of Christ can never be interpreted in terms of bolstering up family life. As the above scriptures show, to follow Christ may mean a family being split up, and, contrary to popular belief over-emphasising the family often causes deep suffering within it.

Perhaps here we should raise an important matter in case there should be misunderstanding. There are some "career Christians" who have interpreted these verses in a selfish way. When they get married they become so absorbed in Christian activity that they seldom see their families, leaving the wife to do all the housework and child caring, and committing her to a life of loneliness and frustration. Such a person should never have got married if he is so unprepared to share life with his partner. The whole of this chapter must be seen and understood in the context of Christian community, which means that every person, married or unmarried, who belongs to Christ, is part of that community. In such a community there are no "career Christians", for all share the life of Christ, and there need then be no lonely and frustrated single or married people. Jesus Himself promised those who lost their homes to follow Him—not a lonely life of isolation, but a new family of love. When Peter said "Lo, we have left our homes and followed you," Jesus replied, "truly I say to you, there is no man who has left house or wife or brothers or parents or children, for the sake of the Kingdom of God, who will not receive *manifold more in this time*, and in the age to come eternal life."[46] Mark in his account elaborates it—"a hundredfold now in this time, houses, and brothers and sisters and mothers and children and lands, with persecutions..."[47] The plurality of houses is an interesting item in this list, in view of the way in which the Church of the Redeemer, Houston, has developed its community life.

There is one further passage which helps to illuminate this subject. It shows how Christ Himself related to his mother and blood brothers on the one hand and his spiritual family on the other. When He was speaking in one place His earthly mother and her other sons called to see Him. When Christ was told this He said, "Who is my mother and who are my brothers?" We are told then that He stretched out His hand towards His disciples and said, "Here are my mother and my brothers! For whoever does the will of my Father in heaven is my brother, and sister, and mother."

These words of Christ indicate that He regarded His relationship to His disciples as being His new "family", and that this family took precedence over the nuclear family. The nuclear family is a temporary relationship. The children will ultimately grow up and leave it, and in heaven there is no marriage—but the inviolable and eternal relationship is that between Christ and His Body, and between brothers and sisters within that Body. Such revolutionary teaching upset the religious people of His day.

As it is easy to be misunderstood (as Jesus Himself was) let us pause and clarify the issues. One is not suggesting free sex or wife swopping. The physical aspects of sex are permissible, in God's sight, only within marriage. Marriage itself is a divine institution, it is a union between two people dissoluble only by death. One is not advocating the weakening in any way of such a relationship. With regard to our parents, the commandment still stands to "honour them". The nuclear family is still God's ordained pattern in which children are to be nurtured. We are still to care for the elderly. But what one is saying is that marriage is not the *only* divine institution, celibacy is too, and Christians may receive a call to be single as well as a call to be married. What one is saying, and Christ's teaching bears this out, is that the nuclear family should not be an exclusive relationship. That our homes should be open-ended, and the highest relationship for the Christian should be that between him and his Lord *and* his brothers and sisters in Christ. So that in practice when we take other Christians into our homes, they are not mere guests, but members of that family, with all that involves as

we shall see in a moment. And in practice far from weakening the family by such an attitude experience shows that it
is greatly strengthened and enhanced. It becomes a very much
healthier place to be than in the exclusive relationships that
most families represent. And once we have grown up and are
free to leave the security of home, whether we are married
or not, we really are free to live our own life and should
never feel obligated to our parents when the prior claims of
God's Kingdom and our brothers and sisters in Christ are
operative. To honour our father and mother does not mean
to "kowtow" to them, live with them, or in any other way to
be necessarily bound to them. As Christians, the relationship
we have with each other is more binding than any human
relationship. These may seem hard words, but it would be
difficult to put any other interpretation on the words spoken
by Christ, such as "He who loves father or mother more than
me is not worthy of me."

Perhaps the most important thing that has been happening
in the Church of the Redeemer, at least as important as anything specifically charismatic, is this new approach to the
family. It is undoubtedly radical and controversial. But if
one examines the whole thing from the vantage point of
scripture, one cannot but conclude that it is much nearer to
the Christian norm than much modern thinking on the
subject. The early Christians not only shared and pooled
their possessions, they shared each other. There are some
who for love's sake may be prepared to "bestow all their goods
to feed the poor"; others "to give their bodies to be burned";
but are we prepared to share our homes and families as a
loving sacrifice, so that further resources may be pooled and
the ministry of the Church extended to a wider circle of
people? That is what Graham Pulkingham and others have
done in Houston, so that there are now over 500 people living
this kind of life. This is how Graham has put it, "God's pro-
vision for successful marriage is that it is to be lived under
the lordship of Jesus Christ, in the power of the Holy Spirit,
in the context of a deeply committed Christian community

turned outward in service to the needs of man ... Most writers on the subject treat the family as an isolated unit for all practical purposes, and tend to be unaware of the transforming power of community life on the family ... This approach, treating the family as an island unto itself, simply expects too much from the family alone, and by and large hasn't worked."[35] As Graham Pulkingham goes on to point out, the Western world has systematically isolated the husband-wife relationship from the rest of society, from the rest of the church, and it is held up as the epitome of true love and fulfilment. So the relationship becomes exclusive. This is a real block to the growth of genuine Christian community. This, as Graham shows in this article in *New Covenant*, not only harms the Body of Christ, which is deprived of so many resources which the family has, but also the family relationship itself. For children growing up in families have to reject them at some point in order to relate freely as persons on their own. But from their early teens many of these young people begin to seek the very same relationship which may have caused them so much misery and unhappiness. Graham writes, "The whole dating, marriage-happiness pattern that dominates our lives is fundamentally distorted. In the plan of God marriage must be seen in the context of community, not as an island in itself."

Graham would be the first to admit that there are massive problems in the way before such a way of life can be established. A husband and wife, for instance, can tolerate many weaknesses and failures in their own relationship to each other. One can learn as the years pass how to get by, without really having to face one another. As Graham says, "Pleasurable times together that re-affirm the relationship compensate for many things. They can go for many years without ever dealing with the hostile and negative aspects of their relationship, living with a perennial frustration and deep down hurt." But when they are called to share their lives together before others, then such problems come to the surface and have to be dealt with. The protective selfish basis of so many relationships is threatened by the Christian community where open sharing in love and the ideal of service is most prominent. Graham writes, "Many of the values associated with marriage are intended to be values lived in the whole Christian community. They have been associated with genital sex and the marriage relationship only as true Christian community has disappeared." He puts his finger on the key to the whole matter when he says, "I don't think that the Lord ever intended for complete self-sufficient community to exist just between two people. I don't mean by this that two people can't establish a very wholesome community, they can; but it seems that the purpose of this kind of relationship is to include others. The fact that in our society marriage has been turned in on itself is causing problems so deep that many couples don't want to face them."[48]

When all this is worked out in practice, the advantages are plain. We have already seen how sharing life together releases time and financial resources for ministry. Opening the home means that many people can have the advantages of a stable home environment, with the love and care that goes with it. The sick and the disabled can be rehabilitated, not in the atmosphere of an institution, but in that of a Christian home. The whole ministry that flows from such households is both flexible and practical enough to meet many situations and personal needs. Many deep emotional problems are caused by bad family relationships. What better way to bring healing than to allow such people the benefit of a true family life.

In spite of man's deep social needs, many people live alone, isolated from the rest of society. Marriage as we have seen is not God's answer either, and even if it was, it is not available to many people anyway. But all may live in community, sharing life to the full. In Houston one knew of many people delivered from deep psychological problems, including forms of sexual perversion, because it was open to them to share in family life, even though they were not married. Modern society is cruel to its bachelors and spinsters, and so are many family people, treating them as "queers" and cruelly assuming frustrations which are basically human and natural, not necessarily sexual. They often want and always need the love and care of other people. But they all too often learn to live with loneliness, and so never develop the full potential of their lives which is possible in community life. Eventually they reach a stage when they cannot face such a life of sharing, and they suffer deeply as a result.

But many would say that such advantages are more than outweighed by the disadvantages, particularly that family life itself suffers, and that the children are unable to take this kind of open-ended life. As a matter of fact the reverse is usually the case. The children of such homes, we found to our surprise, were well above average in the experience of security and in their general well-being. We found them, with very few exceptions, very much happier than the average children we have known who have grown up with a more conventional home life. We saw a much greater unity in the families, the children as well as the parents caring for and being involved in those who needed help and ministry. Like the experience of those brought up in the kibbutz, they seem much better able to relate socially to others, and we saw none of the sullen rebellious kind of young people one often associates with the modern home.

This was confirmed when the Church of the Redeemer was visited by a psychiatrist. The United Presbyterian Church of America set up a commission a few years ago to study the charismatic movement and then report back to the General Assembly. They had a special committee which looked into the psychological implications of the movement. The psychiatrist on the commission, when he visited the Church of the Redeemer, commented that the children from the church were among the most healthy minded he had seen anywhere in America. They were not pre-occupied with thoughts of lust and carnage, and he attributed this to the community environment they were being brought up in, especially the fact that the children seem to have many "fathers" whom they loved and respected. There is no question that they have

a special relationship with their own fathers, but they learn
to accept authority from single men in the same household.

This new way of living means that the Church of the
Redeemer is today like a river overflowing its banks. Fishermen Incorporated is what they officially call the overflow part
of it. It is not a bad name when you consider the many fish
they have incorporated in their large and friendly nets.

9

Fishermen Inc

Christians have become curators of
aquariums rather than fishers of men.
quoted by Dr. George Macleod

IT WAS THE craziest notion Bob had ever had. But he could
not get it out of his mind. Dr. Bob Eckert had an active
medical practice at the time, and was extremely busy. But
the call of God was more and more insistent—"Go to
Mexico." That was all that Bob could get, yet it seemed
preposterous. He had no money to travel that far; his Spanish
was very limited, and in any case Mexico is a big country
and there was no indication *where* he was to go when he got
there, nor what he was to do. But as the weeks passed the call
became more and more definite.

So Bob shared this with his household, and they prayed
about it. He also shared with Bob West who had just come
to Houston from California, and they both felt that God was
calling them to travel together.

When they were in prayer one day, the call to Mexico became more definite and it was impressed upon them that
they should leave on October 14—and they should only take
$300 with them. They were to say nothing about the money
to anyone, but the Lord would provide the finance for the

trip, $268 of which would be spent on their fares. It was then October 1, so they had two weeks to go.

They then began to pray about where they were to go in Mexico. They were at least practical, and bought a map of the country and spread it before the Lord. It was strongly impressed upon them to go to the area known as Chiapas, which is on the borders of Guatemala, and eventually they circled the little village of La Concordia. This was to be the place. But they still didn't know the answer to their question "why". The Lord seemed to be saying "Wait—I'll show you all about that when you get there."

They then shared what they were thinking with a few others, and also with the church fellowship, but without mentioning anything about the money they were needing. About that time $112 was given, followed by a paltry 35c. But the day after the money had been given, and with only a week or so to go before they were due to leave, they met someone who had an immediate and pressing financial need. The $112.35 was given away, so they were back to square one, and a week to go.

Then one morning a gift of $100 came in, $25 of which they had to spend immediately on necessities for the journey. The days went by agonisingly slowly. Still only $75 in the kitty. The last day arrived and they packed to go, and began to say their good-byes.

It was the last night, and the phone bell rang in the Eckert's It was someone who belonged to the Church of the Redeemer.

"Nancy," the voice said, "the Lord's telling me to give Bob $225—do you think he needs it?"

It was a question which did not take very long to answer. And the next day they left for Mexico, without a clue as to why they were going, and with two one-way tickets to the obscure village of La Concordia, and with only a smattering of the Spanish language to communicate with the nationals.

Getting to La Concordia, as it turned out, was no easy matter. The rains had washed away the roads, and the only alternative was to travel on horseback, and that involved Mexican wooden saddles! One puzzle and one problem still remained. The reason for their going was still the burning question, speaking Spanish was still the pressing problem. And when they got there they found that the only interpreter in the area was out of town! But they contacted the local Roman Catholic priest, and with their little Spanish they were able to explain that God had sent them. Whereupon the priest broke down and wept.

"I have been praying for years for God to send a doctor to treat my poor people," he told them. A priest praying in Mexico, a doctor listening in to God in Texas, and the result, a perfect solution.

The two Bobs found the medical situation in a terrible state. Over forty per cent of the children died before they were five years old. Disease and sickness was rampant amongst the Mexicans in the district. There were 20,000 people in this area without a doctor at all.

They found too that the Lord solved the language problem. From their arrival in La Concordia there was a tremendous communication of *love*, rather than language. But within a week God had given to Bob Eckert and Bob West such a grasp of Spanish, that they had no further problems in communicating with the people.

They were quickly able to set up a medical clinic in La Concordia, staffed to begin with by Americans. But within a few years Mexicans had been trained to do the work, so now it is entirely run by Mexicans including a doctor who has become a Christian. When they finally said "good-bye" they were told, "Your words were *evangelisto* [Protestant], but we *saw* that you were Christians." The Mexicans did not say "thank you" so much for the clinic as such, but for those who shared Christ with them. "We want to be like you," they said, "we like your life."

This is only one story of many that could be told of the outreach which has taken place from the Church of the Redeemer. As we have already noticed, there have been two quite distinct periods in the development of this church. The first was when the fellowship itself was being built and established on firm foundations. This was a quiet and secret work. It lasted until 1969. Graham Pulkingham himself spent most of the time in the area of the church, and the inner core of the church spent many hours together. People constantly dropped by and urged them to move out in evangelism, prophesying the direst consequences if they didn't. They listened to these "prophets", but concluded that if God had said that to these people, He certainly hadn't repeated the message to them. They were convinced that God was calling them to stay where they were, to develop strong fellowship, and discover what it really is to be the Body of Christ.

Not that evangelism was entirely neglected. But the church was not going out into the world, instead the Lord was sending the world to them. We have earlier mentioned the steady trickle of people who began to arrive on the doorstep of the church wanting help. They found a warm and open-armed company of people, prepared to spend time and take trouble over them. To pay their debts, put up with their hang-ups, listen to their stories, pray for their needs, share their homes and lead them to Christ and a new way of life in the Body of Christ. Many of the workers in this church today were previously troubled people who came to the church for help.

They believed they had been called to be the Body of Christ, a community of faith-orientated people, who shared a common life. So they avoided anything that would distract them from this task. They neither sought nor encouraged publicity. They kept out of the limelight. They did not get involved in the charismatic movement. They concentrated on the all important task which God had set them.

But in 1969 the second phase or period began. The church started to be "scattered", as the early Christians were. They also began to be known nationally. *Time* magazine described it, for example, as "a viable pattern for the 1970s". Graham was called to travel, and teams started to go out from the church. They have always worked on the principle that "community produces community". In other words, with few exceptions they have gone out from Houston in pairs or groups. Their reasons for doing so include the matter of companionship and safety; but the chief reason is that they can witness corporately, and so encourage others to develop community concepts. From 1969 onwards Graham was away from the church more than he was there. Bob Eckert's trip to Mexico was only one example of the growing outreach. Bill Farra, one of the senior lay leaders, spent a fruitful time helping at St. Paul's Church, Auckland. During this visit the church, whose vicar is Archdeacon Kenneth Prebble, began to take a new direction in its ministry. Attorney Jerry Barker has also travelled extensively and in 1972 settled down in a predominantly black area of Detroit to work alongside the black vicar of an Episcopal church.

In 1969 Fishermen Incorporated was set up, as the outreach arm of the Church of the Redeemer. Its executive director is Gordon Abbott, a friendly and efficient man who wears natty shirts, and looks like the typical American business executive, but behaves very differently.

But even in the area of outreach there are important and significant differences of approach, which makes this apostolic action more like the acts of the old-time apostles than many modern evangelistic techniques and operations. They usually go out in groups, very seldom if ever on their own, and never to work independently of others. This follows the pattern of the apostles who were sent out by our Lord "two by two", as well as Paul and the other apostles who usually travelled and worked in pairs.

Those who have moved out from the Church of the Redeemer have worked on the principle of a total involvement in the life of those they have come to help—and no strings attached. Those who travel live with those to whom they are sent, sharing life fully with them. They have no "empire building" ambitions. They do not set up "branches" of the Redeemer Church. Instead they recognise and respect different expressions of the Body of Christ and dove-tail into them. Their desire is that each work of God should be conformed to Christ's image—rather than patterned on the Redeemer Church itself. The simple style of life which has been adopted by the Redeemer congregation frees many for this kind of ministry; and as the church itself grows in strength, so it is able to share its life with others.

There is a good apostolic precedent for this. The church at Antioch was a powerful and influential one. But when the right time came they did not hesitate to commission their finest leaders and send them out from their fellowship to share Christ with others who were much less privileged.

The Fishermen Incorporated is described as "an instrument of apostolic action". It seeks to work where there is already "a God-given leader". Its object is to "draw out leadership in the church", and "to assist to infiltrate the whole life of the parish". It has many strings to its bow. It has started, for instance, the book and gift shop, alluded to before, in one of the affluent suburbs of Houston, which has been a point of contact with many people and an outlet for service for members of the church community. The organisation also produces stereo records of its choir and the Keyhole singing group. It runs the Coffee House, an outreach to young people which has been instrumental in bringing many to Christ. There are also outreach communities, such as Baldwin House, situated in the hippy district, and Wilson House in the black ghetto. Since 1969 John Grimmet has headed up a work in the county prison. Fishermen Incorporated pay his salary and provide Bibles for distribution to the prisoners. Then there is the Nixon Ranch (no relationship to the President) owned by the church and run by Jerry Arnold, which is an ideal rehabilitation home for men and boys trapped by drugs or crime. It is four hours' drive away from Houston. So one could go on. There is the law office and the medical clinic. There are classes to help the many immigrant Latin Americans speak English. Wherever there is a need, Fishermen try to meet it—whether it is social, moral, physical or spiritual. And the sphere of its influence is spreading wider and wider. They can already say "the world is our parish".

What the Church of the Redeemer has demonstrated, and it is incontrovertible, is the power of the *visible* community to draw people to Christ. The moment the first stones were laid in the foundation of the fellowship; the moment there was a drawing *together* in deep love and commitment to each other, there was also a magnetic drawing of people from outside to the fellowship of Christ and His people. It was as if the magnetic power was switched on the moment the church really became a caring community, and it has continued to draw people ever since.

This is one of the most vital things that the Church needs to learn and develop at the present time, that the power of a visible and collective community will far surpass the sum of that community as individuals. The truth of God needs to be incarnated in human flesh for all to see and hear and touch. People will never see the fullness of Christ in any one individual, only fully in the community of His disciples. One of the most important words that Jesus ever spoke was— "By this all men will know that you are my disciples, if you have love for one another."[49] Disciples become self-evident and recognisable to the world when they begin truly to love one another, and one has to assume that such love is practical, tangible and visible if the world is to see it. It was when the Christians at the Redeemer Church really began to love one another that people around *knew* that they were Christ's people. Their testimony became credible only when their love became visible.

There are two fascinating verses in the New Testament, which when placed alongside each other convey this vital truth. Both John 1:18 and 1 John 4:12 begin with the same words, "No one has ever seen God." Both verses go on to declare how the world is able to see God. In the days of Christ's flesh—it was in Christ Himself—"the only Son, who is in the bosom of the Father, he has made him known." Jesus also put it this way, "He that has seen me has seen the Father." (John 14:9) But in 1 John 4:12 the same words are

followed by these, "If we love one another, God abides in us
and his love is perfected in us." In other words, now that we
can no longer see Christ in His own physical flesh, He is
revealed through the love of Christians for each other. As the
song puts it, "They will know we are Christians by our love,
by our love—yes, they'll know we are Christians by our love."

Another striking aspect of the evangelism of this church
was their appropriation from the start of the power of the
Holy Spirit. Although their love was attractive, it had substance and expression in the gifts of the Holy Spirit. The
sick received more than sympathy and good advice, they were
healed. The confused received words of wisdom and knowledge which were accountable for by the fact that they had
been inspired by the Holy Spirit. The victims of hallucina-
tory drugs were able to return to reality through the power
of the Spirit, others bound by evil forces outside their control
were released by the word of exorcism. Perverts found a
church which believed in a God who could straighten out
the most crooked ways of man. And from the start they found
that community life, sharing closely the life of Christ, and
bringing social misfits and moral perverts within the sphere
of influence of the love of Christ on a day-to-day basis, was
more productive in terms of healing than only counselling
and prayer.

Paul wrote in one of his epistles about a "word only"
gospel. It was not the one that he preached. His message and
his method of presenting it was "in *demonstration* of the
Spirit and power". (1. Cor. 2:4) What he was saying was
seen to be true, because it was supported by the powerful
evidence of signs and wonders. Wherever he preached he
healed the sick, delivered the demon oppressed and showed
by signs and wonders that Jesus Christ was still alive and that
His name was all powerful. But the early church had other
clear-cut evidence to support and demonstrate the veracity
of the word it preached, namely the divinely inspired community, a company of people uniting races and cultures in a
common love and participation, laying down their lives for

one another, having all things in common and sharing a common life as well as a common faith. The attractiveness of the gospel will always be marred and spoilt when either of these two elements are missing. But when they are both present, then the gospel will be, as it was in Paul's day, "the power of God and the wisdom of God".

The unantiseptic risk

To ACCEPT COMMUNITY means to lay down your life. It involves taking risks—without antiseptics. True love is always vulnerable. It can be hurt easily. Community is never easy. It means to allow yourself to be known as you really are, and to let the inevitable abrasive situations turn you into a new person. When the members of the Church of the Redeemer opened their homes to sick members of society, they knew they were taking chances. Psychological disorders can be dangerous. To take a drug addict into your home may spoil the atmosphere and might contaminate others. But love accepts such risks.

Many are talking about "community" at the present time. There was a time when virtually the only Christian communities were the religious orders. Now they are sprouting up all over the world. There are Protestant as well as Catholic ones. They are also one of the important features of the charismatic renewal. The Word of God Community at Ann Arbor, Michigan, which is largely but not exclusively Roman Catholic, and the Barnabas Fellowship at Winterborne

Whitchurch in England, which is largely Anglican, are recent examples. Dr. Francis Schaeffer, who together with his wife Edith, founded the L'Abri Fellowship in Switzerland, writes in his book *The Church at the End of the 20th Century*, "Our churches must be real communities ... they have largely been preaching points and activity generators. Community has had little place ... Every Christian Church ... should be a community which the world may look at as a pilot plant."[50] Elsewhere in the same book he urges Christians to open their homes for community.[51] Father Max Delespesse, who is a Roman Catholic, writes in his book *The Church Community: Leaven and Life-Style*, "Today the Church is certainly tending to become again a community of communities. In all countries we see Christians grouping together into small communities..." According to the same writer, Vatican II will only be able to reach fulfilment "by a return of the Church to its essential form—a community", and he does not regard community life as a special calling for a few people.[52]

What, however, is unusual about the Church of the Redeemer is its new approach to community. Most if not all other communities are special and exceptional groupings of people, set apart from the local church or parish life. Unlike the many hippy communes the Church of the Redeemer is profoundly Christian and Eucharist centred. Unlike the monastic orders it includes families as well as single people. Unlike some of the newer communities, such as Lee Abbey in Britain, Taizé in France, and the Mary Sisters in Germany, it is a local church. Unlike many communities, it has not retreated from the bustle and grime of city life, but is located in the middle of a depressed area of a large city. It is an exciting amalgam of Catholic oriented worship, evangelical outreach, Pentecostal experience, and radical social concern. The church has over forty households who share their lives together, while maintaining the basic unit of the parish and local church. They all gather together for Sunday morning worship. The communities are not exceptional appendages to a stereotype parish structure. The community life is the heart of the church, although membership of a household community is entirely optional. There are few if any local churches which have attempted anything on such a scale as this. But the success of this church can only be explained and understood in terms of this new way of living which has developed over several years.

One of the finest modern exponents of community living was Dietrich Bonhoeffer. One of his most famous cryptic definitions of Christianity was "community through Jesus Christ". In his small book *Life Together* he points to idealism as the greatest hindrance to community life. "Christian brotherhood," he writes, "is not an ideal, but a divine reality. It is a spiritual [geistlich] not a psychic [seelisch] reality." He goes on to say, "A Christian community has broken down because it had sprung from a wish dream ... by sheer grace God will not permit us to live even for a brief period in a dream world ... only that fellowship which faces such disillusionment ... begins to be what it should be in God's sight..."[53] The Church of the Redeemer is not a "dream world". It is composed of realists, many of whom have tasted the bitter fruits of "going it alone" and then having to face their failures and weaknesses before others, only to discover the depths of joy that come from being forgiven. They have found true freedom in laying down their lives for one another. Facing the hard facts of latent selfishness and pride, they have found that when they have shared their life with others a new world of reality has opened up for them.

The story of Jeff O'Connell is a good example of this. It begins with a week night meeting, when unusual thoughts were going through the minds of Jeff and his wife Janellen—all about houses—for home swopping is one of the games they play at the Church of the Redeemer. At the Friday night service Jeff O'Connell was wrestling with a problem. He was sure the Lord was telling him to give their house away. He didn't know why or to whom. But this in itself wasn't the problem. It was how he was going to tell his wife,

Janellen. He eyed her surreptitiously as she sat beside him. She looked so serene. He began to wonder what she'd look like when he spilled the beans. They'd been through deep waters and their home had become a sheltered harbour to them.

Suddenly Janellen leaned over to Jeff:

"You are not going to believe what I'm going to tell you," she said. She too had been wrestling with the same problem and Jeff instinctively knew it—

"Oh yes I am," he said gleefully, "the Lord's telling us to give our house away."

Jeff slipped his hand into Janellen's and gave it an affectionate squeeze.

The weekend passed without their having any idea what this was all about. But their convictions grew. On Tuesday night Jeff attended the elders' meeting. It was there that Dr. Bob Eckert shared with his fellow elders the predicament they had suddenly found themselves in. He and his household, then numbering nineteen people, had been renting a house on the other side of town. Unfortunately the man who owned the property had not been keeping his payments up, so they had suddenly been given a week's notice. They had to be out by that Saturday and had nowhere to go. Jeff knew now why the Lord had given both his wife and himself prior warning.

The elders' meeting begins usually at 10 p.m. and tends to carry on into the early hours. Eventually a jubilant Jeff climbed into bed. Janellen was half awake.

"Guess what the Lord's told us to do?" Jeff whispered.

"You've given our house away," said Janellen, and rolled over and went back to sleep.

This is by no means an unusual story, for this kind of thing happens periodically. The church once had the task of moving no less than five families during one Saturday. What is revealing is the kind of people who do this sort of thing. And Jeff is a case in point.

Jeff had been a "social drinker", which is a nice way of

saying "a drunk". He was at one time a drug salesman whose life was in a mess. He had never really settled in life. He was constantly moving from job to job and city to city. To keep up appearances he began to lie and practise all forms of deceit. It was this which eventually landed him in prison. He became a con man. As his debts built up and his cheques bounced, so he would sell up and move off somewhere else. He was always one jump ahead of his creditors, or almost always.

It was too good to last. On this occasion he had to leave Dallas in a hurry, and so decided to call on an old friend near Galveston, who happened to be Dr. Bob Eckert. He was confident that Bob would believe his carefully fabricated story, and lend him the $200 he needed.

But he was in for a big surprise. In the first place Bob didn't greet him the way he had always done before. And there wasn't the usual double whisky to hand. Something was clearly wrong.

Bob invited Jeff to stay with them, which Jeff gladly accepted. He had nowhere to go anyway. When the right moment came, Jeff spun his usual yarn about the big job which was just coming up, turning on all the charm he could muster.

"You are not telling the truth, you're in trouble," said Bob pointedly. "Besides I don't have any money to give you, I've given it all to the Lord."

Jeff looked as if he had been pole-axed. The last thing he could take was religious stuff.

"Anyway—stay with us," said Bob. Since Jeff only had two dollars to his name he didn't have any alternative.

Jeff came to the Lord while he was there. But his troubles weren't over, nor his sins. Back he went to drink. His whole inclination was to run away rather than face up to his sins. But the day of self-revelation soon dawned, when he realised he was really a coward. That his brash face was a complete sham. He had known many suckers, but Bob wasn't one of them.

He next took a job on a tug-boat, and there his sins finally caught up on him. While working on the tug-boat one day he was told that someone had come to see him. As he disembarked he realised that it was the sheriff with a warrant for his arrest. He was immediately committed to prison pending trial for a series of felonies related to obtaining money under false pretences.

The strange irony of the situation was that going to prison proved to be the means of setting him free. It was the final indignity. He had always been able to pretend before—to live in cloud cuckoo land. But prison was the ultimate reality.

"I felt free for the first time in my life, while I was in jail," is how Jeff explains it. "I knew that the fancy life was over for me, and that I was a coward, a liar, a cheat and a drunkard."

For the first time Jeff knew the meaning of peace. There was *nothing* to do—and there was *nothing* he could do anyway. His soul was at rest.

He spent three weeks in jail. All through this time the Eckerts and the rest of the Redeemer community prayed. Bob's wife Nancy wrote letters of encouragement.

"How can they still love me," Jeff thought to himself.

When he appeared in court he could very easily have received a heavy sentence. He had always been the grand manipulator—finding a way out somehow. But he now found himself doing nothing—just trusting the Lord.

He was found guilty and the moment came for sentence to be given. He stood in the dock in his scruffy prison clothes. He had always chosen his clothes carefully to impress the people he wanted to manipulate. Now it didn't matter any more. His confidence lay somewhere else.

The jury recommended thirty days. The judge, who had a reputation for passing heavy sentences, gave him fifteen days, which meant instant release, as he had already been that length of time in prison before the trial.

Immediately he went back to work to repay all the money he had stolen.

He worked for a time in insurance. "This was difficult," he jokingly told me, "the only people I knew in town were alcoholics and religious fanatics, and neither of these buy much insurance." But he was free at last, and is now one of of the leaders of the Church of the Redeemer. And when the time came and his friend Bob was in need, he willingly gave his house to him. The man who was always manipulating others for his own ends was now laying down his life for them.

In both the Old and New Testaments the household is the basic social entity, and it did not always coincide with the nuclear family. In the Old Testament "the stranger within the gates" was regarded as a beneficiary of the blessings of the covenant, and in the New Testament there are records of household baptism which suggest the same principle. When the jailer at Philippi asked Paul and Silas what he must do to be saved, he was told, "Believe in the Lord Jesus, and you will be saved, *you and your household*." (Acts 16: 31) In Psalm 68:6 God promises to place "the solitary" in families, and in Isaiah 58:7 the fast that God requires includes, "to bring the homeless poor into your house". The home is still today for Jewish people a more important setting for worship than the synagogue, and it seems clear from the Acts of the Apostles that the Church met primarily in homes in the earliest stages of its development. It is probable that this pattern persisted at least until the third century. The household was then the centre of social life, and it was out of the matrix of the home that fellowship and ministry developed. But the household should not be confused with the nuclear family. This is a mistake that has been made in the past in exaggerating the advantages of family life; and thus excluding many from it. Family life has been equated with Christian life.

C. S. Lewis in *The Four Loves* exposes all this. "Were the Victorian novelists right after all?" is the question he asks. "Are the 'domestic affections' when in their best and fullest development, the same thing as the Christian life?" The answer Lewis gives is "certainly not". He goes on, "How many of these 'happy homes' really exist? Worse still; are all the unhappy ones unhappy because affection is absent? I believe not. It can be present, *causing* the unhappiness. Nearly all the characteristics of this love are ambivalent. They may work for ill as well as for good ... The debunkers and anti-sentimentalists have not said all the truth about it, but all they have said is true."[54]

What many have been trying to do is to fit Christianity into the family. What we should have been doing, and what is fundamental in the New Testament, is establishing Christian households, composed of natural family *plus* others, where, to use C. S. Lewis' distinctions, *agape* love is the dominant feature, as well as family love or affection. We have found in Houston that wherever this has taken place, and the nuclear family is fitted into the basic Christian household, the results have been wholly beneficial to the nuclear family.

An interesting example of this fresh approach to marriage in relationship to community is to be found in the Word of God Community in Ann Arbor, Michigan, which has been to some extent modelled on the Church of the Redeemer, Houston. In Ann Arbor one third of the members of the community are young students, for whom marriage and the prospect or otherwise of it plays a large part in their lives. Marriage, so far as they are concerned, is not chosen to satisfy needs that community can meet. But rather it arises out of their union with God and each other as brothers and sisters "in the Lord". John C. Haughey, in an article on the community in the magazine *America,* writes, "Once married, the members have not hewn out for themselves islands of self-sufficiency, but remain an integral part of the community. By doing the opposite, they feel, many American marriages are put in jeopardy because the spouses begin to entertain unreal expectations of one another that can only be satisfied in community. While they are developing this radically different perspective (that community rather than the family constitutes the base on which Christian society must build) they are also learning that what our American culture tries to pass off as marital compatibility is too often an acquiescence in one another's sinfulness. Being part of the community effectively confronts this compromise and gets the spouses beyond the plateau and striving for the holiness to which they are called."[55]

At the Church of the Redeemer they have a much used adage—"Come and live with me and you'll know me." The best way to know a person is to live with them. And the only way to know yourself, and to be yourself, is in relationship to others. The closer these are, the more fulfilled we are. But there is always much pain and change in the process. The marriage relationship on its own cannot achieve the same results, for in marriage there is an exclusive element present, where it cannot legitimately be present in other relationships, and one of the results of this is a touch of permissible unreality. Lovers see each other through rosy-tinted spectacles. But however great an opinion we may have of any other person, when we only know them at a distance, we have only to live with them for a while and any such illusions soon evaporate.

Examining the overall picture of this church over several years one thing is certain, it is a healing community, and most of the deep and lasting therapy has taken place gradually in the day-to-day experience of community life. In an article in the *Sunday Times* on suicide entitled 'Last Resort', G. M. Carstairs, Professor of Psychological Medicine at Edinburgh University, wrote that the two social factors most clearly associated with high rates of suicide were social isolation and geographical mobility—in other words, lack of community. The interesting thing is that in wartime suicide rates fall dramatically. Carstairs comments, "War conditions recreate, to a considerable extent, that sense of solidarity, of sharing with one's neighbours and of submitting to a common discipline *which used to characterise traditional pre-industrial communities.*"[56] The truth of this can also be seen in the apparent fall in mental sickness in Northern Ireland during the present troubles.

But suicide or attempted suicide are not the only mental states of mind which are the product of the breakdown of community living. A person who takes his own life has been pressed to the ultimate. Thousands of others, suffering from what Carstairs in the same article calls "the diseases of civilisation," such as, anxiety states, neuroses and psycho-somatic disorders, live in agonising misery, even though sur-rounded by and indulging in the accepted norms of affluence, because our modern society has murdered community, and provided no satisfactory replacement. In the Church of the Redeemer, hundreds of people have discovered that com-munity, for all its pains, has brought healing and freedom from the mental diseases of our so-called civilisation. It is probably true to say that community living is the only really satisfactory solution to many of these disorders.

Visitors to the Church of the Redeemer are immediately made welcome in the rather unconventional manner of a physical embrace—without respect to age or sex. Some object to this custom. During the Sunday morning Eucharist, at the Kiss of Peace, members of the church embrace the people close to them, and sometimes leave their seats to show their affection by hugging friends and strangers alike. This poses real problems for those brought up in the prim and proper traditions in which a warm handshake and perhaps an arm round the shoulder is the furthest one can usually go to express love for others. The whole business has all kinds of taboos attached to it. Do we not need to be liberated from Anglo-Saxon coldness and prudery? C. S. Lewis has no place for such attitudes. He writes, "Kisses, tears and embraces are not in themselves evidence of homosexuality. The implica-tions would be, if nothing else, too comic. Hrothgar embrac-ing Beowulf, Johnson embracing Boswell (a pretty flagrantly heterosexual couple) and all those hairy old toughs of centurions in Tacitus, clinging to one another and begging for last kisses when the legion was broken up ... all pansies? If you can believe that you can believe anything. On a broad historical view it is, of course, not the demonstrative gestures of friendship among our ancestors but the absence of such gestures in our own society that calls for some special explanation. *We, not they, are out of step.*"[57] The same writer in his Narnia saga *The Lion, the Witch and the Wardrobe*, describes the scene when Susan and Peter meet, "I won't say there wasn't kissing and crying on both sides. But in Narnia no-one thinks any the worse of you for that."[58] Some may argue there are dangers in such goings on, and that they can be the first steps on a slippery pathway. All one can say is that there is no evidence of this in Houston. History, as C. S. Lewis has written, and common sense is on their side. One has sometimes wondered what would happen if we took seriously the words of the famous carol 'God rest you merry gentlemen' and acted on them,

> Now to the Lord sing praises
> All you within this place,
> And with true love and brotherhood,
> Each other now embrace.

Why not?

When Jeanne and I visited the church in 1972 we made a special point of seeing some of the many household communities. We had lunch with Essie Ringo in her home on McKinney Street (renamed All Saints Street by members of the church as so many of the houses are now owned by them). Essie's ministry is to care for abandoned or neglected children. At that time she was looking after eleven children under twelve years old. She also had nine adults living in the house and forming part of her household community. We met Tommy, an autistic child, who is beginning to experience healing in the loving security of a Christian home. He has now started to speak and communicate with those around him.

One of the more recent communities is called Wilson House. It is situated in the heart of the black quarter. Next door is the headquarters of the black panthers. The area is thickly impregnated with the atmosphere of violence and corruption. Voodooism is practised openly. Alcoholism is rampant. Threats and assaults take place regularly. Into that area moved members of the Redeemer Church. Their leader is Charles High, a black who is a brilliant pianist. It is a mixed community of blacks and whites. Together in Christian love and followship they work out the tensions and problems of racial integration. Their light cannot be hidden, nor their darkness. The houses have their walls, and the neighbours hear everything. They hear their songs and their prayers, their quarrels and their angry moments. In the small living room the heroes of under-privileged America look down upon them—Martin Luther King and Jack and Robert Kennedy, all dead from assassins' bullets. While we were there one of the black panthers called in. He could see for himself that it can be done, blacks and whites can live together in Christ.

We had dinner in Baldwin House, situated in the hippy district. We enjoyed a pork joint which had been given them, a treat and change from the usual simple fare. Here a ministry is carried on amongst the hippies. We sat cross-legged on the floor afterwards and sang songs together. A Christian group called Symphony of Souls, which was then travelling in a bus across the United States led us in songs of their own accompanied by the wierdest oriental instruments, which they had mastered without tuition.

There are many different types of household communities, and they are constantly changing. New ones are being added. Some old ones close down when there is no longer any need for them, others change their character as people come and go and new needs arise. Mostly the communities cater for a particular need. Some concentrate on rehabilitating emotionally disturbed people, others on supporting a particular ministry of the church, such as the coffee house or medical clinic. Other needy people who are helped in the households include drug addicts, delinquent teenagers, unmarried mothers, old folk, mentally retarded people, and the physically handicapped. There is assuredly a home somewhere for "the lame, the halt and the blind".

There is no common rule of life to cover all the households. Every household has its own. But each one has found it necessary to have certain disciplines, but based on the law of love. Every household has a head. Normally there is only one nuclear family per household, so the head is usually the husband. In other households where there is no nuclear family the head may be a woman. The heads of the various households meet regularly to compare notes and share together. They all back each other up. They are limbs and members of one Body. The households are constantly changing as people come and go. Graham Pulkingham himself moved with his wife and children from the Rectory to the Way In coffee house. Later they moved again to a house in an integrated area near the University, a very much larger and finer property. But in 1972 they pulled their roots up again and crossed to England where they have set up home in a house on a Coventry housing estate.

Jerry Barker describes their community life as "living the Christian life within a house in such a way that it can be seen and experienced by people in the neighbourhood". The contrast of this life with the world around is so stark and obvious that it makes people think much more radically than if they had only been able to listen to sermons. Some people are threatened by such blatantly obvious Christianity, because, as Jerry has put it, "It convinces them that it is *possible* to live the Lord's life, that it is *possible* to love each other, that it is *really possible* to live by the power God has given to man to live by His Spirit." Harvey Cox in one of his books has prophesied, "The visible *style* of the church's life will become a much more significant element in the communication of the gospel ... it means the church may become the *verbum visibile*, the visual enactment of the message it bears in a newly important way." He goes on in the McLuhan style to say, "In a culture increasingly dependent on visual parables and signs for its orientation to the world, the conduct of the Christian community, its visible behaviour, will become a much more significant 'word' than the pronouncements of the pulpit."[59]

Every night Jerry and his household have "open house". People are encouraged to drop in as friends do. They gather in the living room and share about what the Lord is doing in their lives. "We relate everything to faith," Jerry explains, "we talk faith, we relate to each other in faith." So as not to catch people off guard, a hand-shake usually does for the first visit. But then they openly embrace one another with a big hug. Many of the black people in the neighbourhood have never known that kind of a relationship with the whites.

Perhaps the major contribution that the Church of the Redeemer has made to the Church at large is that it has demonstrated that the practice and experience of community can be easily available to everyone. Community is not easy. But this church has shown that it need no longer be practised by a few dreamy-eyed idealists; nor need it be something special and removed from the rest of the Church. But the local church can become "a community of communities", catering for the needs of an entire neighbourhood. Each household can act as one effective member of the one Body—the local church. So a ministry builds up which is flexible enough to cope with changing situations and fresh needs as they arise. It is a break-through of immense importance for the future of the Church everywhere.

II

Songs of fellowship

WHAT IS IT that draws people to this church and has made it a mecca for so many brands of Christianity? Heinz 57 varieties isn't in it when you attend the Friday night open fellowship. Every kind of Christian comes along from Southern Baptist fundamentalists to way out radicals. They're all there—wide-eyed and on tip-toe. Basically, I suppose it is because the Church of the Redeemer is such a synthesis of different strands of Christian tradition that most people feel at home. It's what so many people have longed for. You'll find there a Catholic sense of community, with a respect for and enjoyment of the sacraments, particularly Holy Communion. There is a daily noon Communion service which draws people like a magnet. Bill Hosford, a business-man, came twenty miles to a mid-day Eucharist to find out what it was all about, and continued coming every day for the next three months. But the Catholic element is lively and unfussy. Worship is not a ritual and grace is not mechani-cal. There is no place for a shallow churchianity. And this element of the life of the Church of the Redeemer does not clash with the other ones. Catholics do not imagine they have strayed into the Bible punching fundamentalist camp. They don't feel out of place.

But the "finger-in-his-Bible" Christian is pleasantly surprised when he attends the Church of the Redeemer. He knows what the score is. He's looking for faults and has chapter and verse ready. But he finds a church that is orthodox enough for anyone, even Southern Baptists. He discovers church members know their Bibles—many attend the daily "Bible-sharing group". He is glad to see as dedicated a group of people as you will find anywhere—and there is no sense that they are a religious club, concerned only with the preservation of their piety. Religious people can be adept at talking. But these Christians don't just talk their faith, they face up to the realities of life and do something about it. Moreover with their strong emphasis on community this church has not been ensnared by individualism, nor is there anything dull or prosaic about their approach to life. They are open to God working in any and every situation. Miracles are quietly happening all the time, and this does not surprise them.

But Pentecostals, too, find common ground. They are pleasantly surprised to find that the gifts of the Holy Spirit are in evidence at the heart of the church's life. The sick are prayed for. Prophesyings are heard. Speaking in tongues is practised by many of the church members, and in the services singing in tongues is a fairly frequent experience: spontaneously the Holy Spirit gives to several people words and music, and the results are usually quite breath-taking. "Hallelujahs" are often on the lips, and "praise the Lord" is a phrase you'll hear many times over as the members of this church talk informally and share what God has been doing in their lives. But this brand of Pentecostalism is refreshingly free from any kind of sectarian spirit or hint of spiritual superiority. They are people who express their freedom in worship and praise, but do not allow such freedom to degenerate into undisciplined behaviour. When the

Bishop of the diocese visited the church one Sunday one of the younger choirmen began to sing in tongues and the whole congregation joined in. Most Anglican churches tend to be a little over-awed when their father in God is present, and the Church of the Redeemer is no exception. Graham Pulkingham was a little apprehensive about what the Bishop would say about this departure from Episcopal "decency" and decorum. He need not have worried. "A nice service," the Bishop said as he disrobed in the vestry afterwards—"I'm always so fond of your music. I particularly liked that little anthem the choirman began to sing..."

One of the tragic dichotomies of the modern Church is between those who stress the social aspects of the Gospel, and minimise the spiritual, and others who stress the spiritual and largely leave out the social. The secular theologians have had a good innings and perhaps are now waning in influence. On the other hand, the Achilles heel of anything Pentecostal is usually such a strong emphasis on the spiritual that concern for the world is seen exclusively in terms of evangelism. But the Church of the Redeemer has never polarised itself in these ways. Its strong emphasis on worship and the knowledge and experience of the Fatherhood of God, the Lordship of Christ and the power of the Spirit, have not diverted the attention of its members from the world's needs; and the church has seen itself responsible for such matters as education, medical care, legal aid, in their neighbourhood, *as well as* bringing men and women to Christ and the fellowship of His Church. And its concern to clothe the naked, feed the hungry, bind up the wounded, defend the victims of injustice and visit the prisoners has never been divorced from their faith in God and their desire to express it in worship.

Harvey Cox has written, "The church is a singing as well as a marching community"; and that certainly describes this church. When Betty Jane Pulkingham, the Rector's wife, attended her very first service in the Church of the Redeemer she was struck by the last line of Psalm 150, "Let everything that hath breath, praise the Lord." From that moment onwards God gave her a strong ambition to see the whole body of believers of the church expressing praise to God in joyful harmony. This was later to come to pass, but like everything else that developed in the church it sprang out of their community life, and became their most free and united expression of what it meant to them in terms of love for God and appreciation of each other. In Romans 15:5-6 Paul expresses this aptly. He writes of Christians living "in such harmony with one another, in accord with Christ Jesus" that they might express this harmony—"that together you may with one voice glorify the God and Father of our Lord Jesus Christ". They have found that the harmony and peace discovered in sharing life together has radically affected the quality of their singing. The two belong together. No amount of skilful training or natural musical talent can substitute for the harmony of human relationships—and yet training matters as God showed Betty Jane through another scripture, Psalm 33:3, "Play *skilfully* with a loud noise."

In his autobiography, Dr. Matthews, the former Dean of St. Paul's Cathedral, has written about music, "I believe that the unifying power of music has not been exploited to the full. There are untried possibilities. When we can use each other's music freely and hopefully, we shall be on the way to unity of the Spirit."[60]

The unity of the Spirit in any church does depend on a mutual acceptance of one another and this applies very much to the musical aspects. In the Church of the Redeemer professional musicians and the untrained have made music together. This has not been easy for the professional. Gary Miles was a young tenor who came into the choir as a paid singer. But after being baptised in the Holy Spirit during a Sunday Eucharist, he turned in his pay cheque! For a time Gary struggled to reconcile his sophisticated musical tastes with the simple fare of Pentecostal choruses which were then being sung by the growing community at small chapel services and informal home meetings—where there were no instruments to accompany the great hymns used on Sundays.

In such a setting, simple rhythmic choruses served a useful purpose in the offering of praise. Gary was particularly offended by the chorus "power in the blood". But one day the Lord brought to his musical imagination three completely new verses for it! He could no longer despise this song, and the depth and beauty of the new verses have brought to many a completely fresh appreciation for this well-known chorus. In a similar experience, Kathleen Thomerson, who was organist at the church for a time and composer of many songs, was inspired to write a chorale-prelude using as the *cantus firmus* in the pedals the melody of "Turn your eyes on Jesus"—a chorus at which she had demurred only the week before!

Jeanne and I will always remember the first Sunday we attended the Eucharist at the Church of the Redeemer. According to the book of Revelation music figures prominently in heaven, and we felt that we had experienced a foretaste that day. There was a gentleness about the whole service, particularly the singing, and yet a joyful spontaneity that was most liberating. We had some of the old hymns, a few songs of their own composition, and the *Melchizedek Mass*, a liturgical setting for the Holy Communion written by Betty Jane, which beautifully combines organ and guitars in the accompaniment. Here for sure was good music, yet simple enough for all to join in. The music, competent in itself, was yet so infused with the Spirit of God that it lifted us up to Him in adoration and praise such as we had seldom experienced.

It is interesting that the late Karl Barth used to listen to music every morning as part of his preparation for theological study, writing and teaching. Dr. Martyn Lloyd-Jones in his book *Preaching and Preachers*[61] acknowledges his own debt to music as part of his preparation for preaching. If those who preach and teach have found a valuable place for music in their preparation, the Church of the Redeemer has also come to emphasise the part it plays in preparing worshippers for the ministry of God's Word. We saw fellowship and joy come, and the people turn refreshed to listen to the Word.

Someone has said that every Christian has within him the latent ability to write at least one good hymn. Whether this is true or not, the fact remains that when we receive the Spirit, He is the Creator Spirit, and so it was no surprise that we found in the Church of the Redeemer people who have become creative in many directions, of which music is only one.

The whole of life has become for them the raw material out of which songs are born. A happy-go-lucky bus trip across country inspired "Sing, sing Alleluia", a song for the coffee house singing group. The challenge of waking lots of children cheerfully in the morning prompted "Wake up, wake up", a song which incorporates much Advent teaching. David Pulkingham's "nanny" received a song on his fourth birthday, the subject matter of which was King David's early life. A young university voice instructor sang a powerful message to students who regarded peace as the absence of war, "They say that peace is never bought by bloodshed; peace is never won in war. But I know that everlasting peace was bought by the blood of one Man."

In the Church of the Redeemer music is the principle expression of their corporate life. If they have found a new way of living, then they have certainly found a new way of expressing it.

References

1 Hodder and Stoughton 1973
2 Collins 1971, p. 9
3 *The Future of the Christian Church* by Michael Ramsey, Archbishop of Canterbury and Leon-Joseph Suenens (SCM Press 1970), p. 53
4 Quoted in *Future Shock* by Alvia Toffler (Bodley Head 1970), p. 96-97
5 Ibid, p. 325
6 SCM Press 1968, p. 55
7 John 12:24
8 Proverbs 11:14
9 Doubleday 1965
10 *Why Bishops?*, p. 9
11 Tyndale House, November 1972
12 *Why Bishops?*, p. 19
13 Ibid, p. 19
14 Published in Britain by the Fountain Trust
15 Luke 14:16-24
16 Luke 12:15
17 Matthew 6:19-21
18 Luke 12:22f
19 Romans 14:17
20 Luke 6:20 cf Matthew 5:3
21 Luke 6:24-25
22 Acts 5:4

23 Acts 2:44-45
24 Acts 4:32-35
25 Quoted in *The Church Community: Leaven and Life-Style* by Max Delespesse (Catholic Centre St Paul University, 1968), p. 40-41
26 Ibid, p. 40-41
27 Ibid, p. 42-43
28 *On not leaving it to the Snake*, p. 133
29 1 John 3:17-18
30 *New Covenant* magazine December 1971, p. 7
31 Luke 9:59
32 1 Corinthians 7:7
33 *Time* magazine December 28, 1970
34 Macmillan 1971
35 *New Covenant* magazine December 1971, p. 11
36 Collins 1960, p. 48
37 2 Timothy 3:2
38 *Memories and Meanings*, Hodder and Stoughton 1969, p. 15
39 Matthew 22:29
40 Matthew 19:10-12
41 In a discussion with Graham Pulkingham he put forward the view that marriage and celibacy were both gifts *to* rather than *from* God. For both are a matter of choice and commitment rather than of special grace. So Paul thought it lawful for him to marry, but for the Kingdom's sake wanted all men to be as himself.
42 *The Four Loves*, p. 89
43 Matthew 4:22
44 Matthew 10:34f
45 Luke 14:26
46 Luke 18:28
47 Mark 10:29-31
48 *New Covenant* magazine December 1971, p. 13
49 John 13:35
50 Norfolk Press 1970, p. 50-51
51 p. 130
52 p. 21-22, 56-57
53 SCM Press, p. 15
54 *The Four Loves*, p. 39
55 February 12, 1972, p. 143
56 *Sunday Times*
57 *The Four Loves*, p. 59-60
58 Geoffrey Bles 1950 (Puffin edition, p. 121)
59 *On not leaving it to the Snake*, p. 28
60 *Memories and Meanings*, p. 19
61 Hodder and Stoughton 1971, p. 183